The Power® Of:
Financial Calculations for Multiplan™

by

Robert E. Williams

A SPECTRUM BOOK

Prentice-Hall, Inc., Englewood Cliffs, New Jersey 07632

Management Information Source, Inc.

10 9 8 7 6 5 4 3 2 1

ISBN 0-13-687112-7

ISBN 0-13-687724-9

Edited by: Estelle Phillips

ONE OF A SERIES OF INSTRUCTION MANUALS ON THE USE AND
APPLICATION OF COMPUTER PROGRAMS

The Power Of: ™ is a trademark of Management Information Source, Inc.

Distributed by Prentice-Hall, Inc., Englewood Cliffs, New Jersey 07632.
A Spectrum Book. Printed in the United States of America.

This book is available at a special discount when ordered in bulk quantities. Contact Prentice-Hall, Inc., General Publishing Division, Special Sales, Englewood Cliffs, N.J. 07632.

Prentice-Hall International, Inc., *London*
Prentice-Hall of Australia Pty. Limited, *Sydney*
Prentice-Hall Canada Inc., *Toronto*
Prentice-Hall of India Private Limited, *New Delhi*
Prentice-Hall of Japan, Inc., *Tokyo*
Prentice-Hall of Southeast Asia Pte. Ltd., *Singapore*
Whitehall Books Limited, *Wellington, New Zealand*
Editora Prentice-Hall do Brasil Ltda., *Rio de Janeiro*

PREFACE

The Power Of: Financial Calculations for Multiplan presents practical solutions to everyday problems facing the businessman. The purpose of this book is to aid in the many decision-making situations that face business people daily.

The emphasis in The Power Of: Financial Calculations for Multiplan is on presenting the solutions to real-life problems, rather than concentrating on explanations of theories and formulas.

Multiplan's NAME command has been employed in almost every chapter in order to simplify the entry of the sometimes lengthy formulas. For clarity in understanding where formulas are to be entered, the formula(s) in each exercise is displayed in an adjacent area in a box with an arrow pointing to the cell into which the formula is to be entered.

No special training is needed to benefit from this book. All the instructions are in plain English. The procedures necessary to perform each exercise are given to the reader in a step-by-step manner.

The Power Of: Financial Calculations for Multiplan will become your most valuable reference book in solving financial problems.

**IF YOU OWN, OR ARE THINKING OF OWNING, MULTIPLAN,
YOU SHOULD OWN THIS BOOK!**

INTRODUCTION

This book has been purposely designed to provide an opportunity to easily follow the logic of Multiplan functions, and then apply those functions to specific problem-solving situations. Each chapter is self-contained. Each demonstrates some special ability or abilities we have used in solving problems.

The Multiplan format is arranged on the computer screen in columns and rows. The Multiplan format is illustrated in Figure 1. The columns and rows are identified by number designations. Each position where a column and row intersect is a cell, or location, as on a street map. The relationships between the values in these cells are determined by simple instructions entered into the cells in the form of algebraic formulas. (Don't get panicky; that just means (a + b) and other similar expressions.) Visualizing the street map image and following the exercises, you will easily and quickly catch on to the power of Multiplan and how it can work for you.

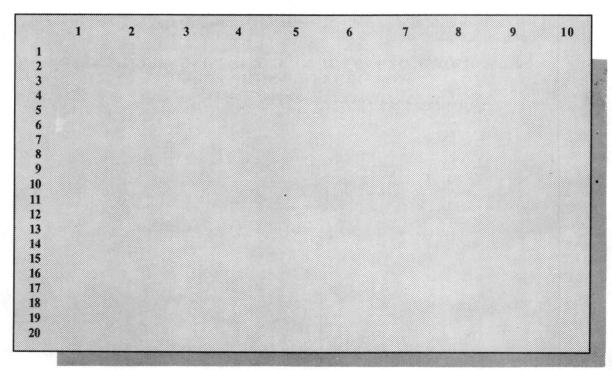

Figure 1

FINANCIAL CALCULATIONS
TABLE OF CONTENTS

CHAPTER ONE

AMORTIZATION SCHEDULE

DESCRIPTION

An amortized loan is one which is liquidated on an installment basis, i.e., the principal amount of the loan is repaid in installments during the life of the loan.

This amortization schedule will find an unknown payment amount from a known principal amount. It will also calculate an unknown principal amount from a known payment amount.

From this information, a report is generated which contains the term, the interest payment, principal payment, the principal still owing, and the interest and the principal paid to date on the loan.

EXAMPLE

FINDING THE UNKNOWN PAYMENT FROM A KNOWN PRINCIPAL
(Illustrated in Figure 1)

The principal of a loan is $3,145. The interest is 12%, the number of compounding periods per year is 12, the number of payments per year is 12, and the total payments are 20.

What is the amount of each payment?

FINDING THE UNKNOWN PRINCIPAL FROM A KNOWN PAYMENT
(Illustrated in Figure 2)

The payment on a loan is $200. The interest is 14%, the number of compounding periods per year is 12, the number of payments per year is 12, and the total payments are 10.

What is the amount of the principal?

SETTING UP YOUR WORKSHEET - ENTERING LABELS (Figure 1)

USE THE FOLLOWING STEP-BY-STEP DIRECTIONS FOR ENTERING THE LABELS IN FIGURE 1:

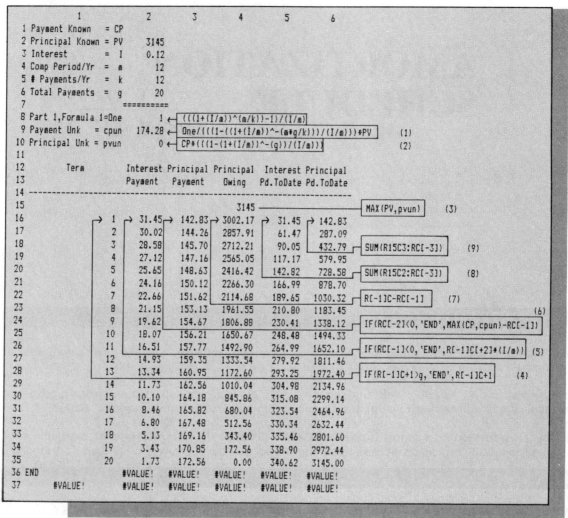

Figure 1

Finding the Unknown Payment from a Known Principal

Before you type in your labels, you need to expand column 1 to allow for the long labels. To do this,

Place your cursor on column 1 and type:

F	starts FORMAT command
W	selects Width option
20	column width
RETURN	executes the command

AFTER READING THE FOLLOWING NOTES, type in your labels.

NOTE

Before typing in labels, you must first type:

A   starts ALPHA command which prepares the
                     cell for labeling information

Then type in the label.

RETURN   enters label

NOTE

DO NOT TYPE in the word "END" in row 36. The word will
automatically appear later in the exercise, as the result of a formula which you will be entering later in this exercise.

Now enter your labels.

After entering your labels, you will want to center the labels in rows 12 and 13. To do this,

Place your cursor on R12C1 and type:

F   starts FORMAT command

C   selects Cells option and displays R12C1

:   colon - indicates from-to

R13C6   last cell to format

TAB   moves cursor to Alignment

C   selects Center option

RETURN   executes the command

To enter the double-dashed line in row 7,

Place your cursor on R7C2 and type:

A   starts ALPHA command

= = = = = = = = = = 10 equal signs (=)

RETURN   executes the command

To enter the single dashed line in row 14,

Place your cursor on R14C1 and type:

A	starts ALPHA command
--------------------	20 dashes (-)
RETURN	executes the command

To copy the single-dashed line across the row,

Leave your cursor on R14C1 and type:

C	starts COPY command
R	selects Right option
5	number of columns to copy into
RETURN	executes the command

After you have entered all the labels, you will begin entering the known values and naming their locations.

ENTERING AND NAMING VALUES

USE THE FOLLOWING STEP-BY-STEP DIRECTIONS FOR ENTERING AND NAMING THE KNOWN VALUES:

NOTE

Naming of cells or groups of cells where values or formulas are placed is only done to make it easier to describe the cells' locations when used in formulas. If you don't name the cells, you can type in the address or point to the cell for cell identification.

Once a cell or a group of cells is named, the name remains, regardless of any labels, values or formulas that may be entered into that location.

In this exercise, we have taken the option of naming some of the cells in order to make the construction of the formula(s) easier to understand.

BEFORE YOU BEGIN entering and naming the known values, you will name the BLANK cell in column 2, to the right of CP, Payment Known.

To name the BLANK cell in column 2, to the right of CP,

Place your cursor on R1C2 and type:

N	starts NAME command
CP	name given to cell
RETURN	executes the command

Now you will enter and name the known values.

The first value to enter in column 2, to the right of PV, is the known principal amount.

Place your cursor on R2C2 and type:

3145	principal
RETURN	enters the value

Now you will name the cell into which you have just entered the value.

Leave your cursor on R2C2 and type:

N	starts NAME command
PV	name given to cell
RETURN	executes the command

The second value in column 2, to the right of I, is the interest percent.

Place your cursor on R3C2 and type:

0.12	interest percent
RETURN	enters the value

Now you will name the cell into which you have just entered the value.

Leave your cursor on R3C2 and type:

N	starts NAME command
I	name given to cell
RETURN	executes the command

The third value in column 2, to the right of m, is the number of compounding periods per year.

Place your cursor on R4C2 and type:

12	number of compounding periods per year.
RETURN	enters the value

Now you will name the cell into which you have just entered the value.

Leave your cursor on R4C2 and type:

N	starts NAME command
m	name given to cell
RETURN	executes the command

The fourth value in column 2, to the right of k, is the number of payments made per year.

Place your cursor on R5C2 and type:

12	number of payments made per year.
[RETURN]	enters the value

- Now you will name the cell into which you have just entered the value.

Leave your cursor on R5C2 and type:

N	starts NAME command
k	name given to cell
[RETURN]	executes the command

The fifth value in column 2, to the right of g, is the total number of payments.

Place your cursor on R6C2 and type:

20	total number of payments
[RETURN]	enters the value

Now you will name the cell into which you have just entered the value.

Leave your cursor on R6C2 and type:

N	starts NAME command
g	name given to cell
[RETURN]	executes the command

Now that you have entered all the known values, you will enter the formulas.

ENTERING FORMULAS

USE THE FOLLOWING STEP-BY-STEP DIRECTIONS FOR ENTERING THE FORMULAS WHICH WILL CALCULATE THE UNKNOWN VALUES, and name them if the values generated by them are needed in another formula.

NOTE

Multiplan will not accept FORMULA ONE in its entirety, because it has too many words. As a result, we have to break the formula into two parts. Therefore, the procedure for entering FORMULA ONE will be different from the usual procedure.

Follow the step-by-step directions carefully for entering FORMULA ONE.

Formula one in column 2, to the right of cpun, calculates the unknown payment.

Enter the first part of formula one, in column 2, immediately underneath the double-dashed line, to the right of One. To do this,

Place your cursor on R8C2 and type:

$(((1 + (I / m)) ^ (m / k)) - 1) / (I / m)$ first part of formula one

RETURN   enters the first part of formula one

Now you will name the first part of formula one. To do this,

Leave your cursor on R8C2 and type:

N   starts NAME command

One   name given to cell

RETURN   executes the command

Now you will be able to enter formula one, in column 2, to the right of cpun, which will calculate the Unknown Payment. To do this,

Place your cursor on R9C2 and type:

V   starts VALUE command

One   part one of formula one

/   divides

$(((1 - ((1 + (I / m)) ^ - (m * g / k))) / (I / m))) * PV$ part two of formula one

RETURN   enters formula one

You now need to format the cell so that it will be displayed with two decimal places. To do this,

Leave your cursor on R9C2 and type:

F   starts FORMAT command

C   selects Cells option and displays R9C2

TAB TAB   moves cursor to Format Code:

F   selects Fixed option

TAB   moves cursor to # of decimals:

2   number of decimal places

RETURN   executes the command

Now you will name the cell into which you have just entered formula one. To do this,

Leave your cursor on R9C2 and type:

N   starts NAME command

cpun   name given to cell

RETURN   executes the command

Formula two in column two, to the right of pvun, will calculate the unknown principal.

```
_____ NOTE _____

This formula will be utilized later in the exercise, when
calculating the unknown principal as shown in Figure 2.

You will enter the formula now, so that it will be ready to do the
calculations necessary later in this exercise.
```

To enter formula two, in column 2, to the right of pvun, which will calculate the unknown principal,

Place your cursor on R10C2 and type:

V   starts VALUE command

CP * (((1 — (1 + (I / m))^ — (g)) / (I / m)))   formula

RETURN   enters the formula

Now you will name the cell into which you have just entered the formula.

Leave your cursor on R10C2 and type:

N   starts NAME command

pvun   name given to cell

RETURN   executes the command

Formula three, in column 4, immediately underneath the single dashed line, in the Principal Owing column, is the amount of principal still owing.

Place your cursor on R15C4 and type:

V   starts VALUE cómmand

MAX(PV,pvun)   formula

RETURN   enters the formula

Formula four, is in column one, the Term column.

Place your cursor on R16C1 and type:

V	starts VALUE command
IF (	starts IF function and opens expression
[UP ARROW]	moves cursor up one cell and displays R[-1]C
+	adds
1 > g, "END",	if Term is greater than g, then "END" will be displayed.
[UP ARROW]	moves cursor up one cell and displays R[-1]C
+ 1)	adds 1 and closes expression
[RETURN]	enters the formula

Formula five is in column 2, in the Interest Payment column.

Place your cursor on R16C2 and type:

V	starts VALUE command
IF (	starts IF function and opens expression
[LEFT ARROW]	moves cursor to first year (1) and displays R[-1]C
< 0, "END",	if Term is less than 0, then "END" will be displayed
[UP ARROW]	
[RIGHT ARROW] [RIGHT ARROW]	moves cursor to Principal Owing and displays R[-1]C[+ 2]
*	multiplies
(I/m)	interest divided by number of compounding periods per year.
)	closes expression
[RETURN]	enters the formula

Formula six is in column 3, the Principal Payment column.

Place your cursor on R16C3 and type:

V	starts VALUE command
IF (	starts IF function and opens expression
[LEFT ARROW]	
[LEFT ARROW]	moves cursor to Term (1) and displays RC[-2]

< 0, "END",MAX(CP,cpun)	If the term is less than 0, then "END" will be displayed; otherwise the MAX function will select the CP (the Known Payment) or the cpun (the Unknown Payment)
—	subtracts
LEFT ARROW	moves cursor to Interest Payment and displays RC[-1]
)	closes IF function
RETURN	enters the formula

Formula seven is in column 4, the Principal Owing column.

Place your cursor on R16C4 and type:

V	starts VALUE command
UP ARROW	moves cursor to Principal Owing and displays R[-1]C
—	subtracts
LEFT ARROW	moves cursor to Principal Payment and displays RC[-1]
RETURN	enters the formula

Formula eight is in column 5, the Interest Paid To Date column.

Place your cursor on R16C5 and type:

V	starts VALUE command
SUM (	starts SUM function and adds values in the following list
R15C2	first value in list to add
:	colon - indicates from-to
LEFT ARROW	
LEFT ARROW	
LEFT ARROW	moves cursor to last value in list to add, and displays RC[-3]
)	closes expression
RETURN	enters the formula

Formula nine is in column 6, the Principal Paid To Date column.

Place your cursor on R16C6 and type:

V	starts VALUE command

SUM (	starts SUM function and adds values in the following list
R15C3	first value in list to add
:	colon - indicates from-to
⬚ LEFT ARROW	
⬚ LEFT ARROW	
⬚ LEFT ARROW	moves cursor to last value in list to add, and displays RC[-3]
)	closes expression
⬚ RETURN	enters the formula

Now you will need to format the cells into which you have just entered formulas 5, 6, 7, 8 and 9, in Row 16, so that they will be displayed with 2 decimal places. To do this,

Place your cursor on R16C2 and type:

F	starts FORMAT command
C	selects Cells option and displays R16C2, first cell to format
:	colon - indicates from-to
R16C6	last cell to format
⬚ TAB ⬚ TAB	moves cursor to Format Code:
F	selects Fixed option
⬚ TAB	moves cursor to # of decimals:
2	number of decimal places
⬚ RETURN	executes the command

Now you will copy all the formulas you have just entered into row 16 down their respective columns. To do this,

Place your cursor on R16C1 and type:

C	starts COPY command
F	selects From option and displays R16C1, first cell to copy from
:	colon - indicates from-to
R16C6	last cell to copy from
⬚ TAB	moves cursor to To Cells: and displays R16C1, first cell to copy to

:	colon - indicates from-to
R37C1	last cell to copy to
RETURN	executes the command

_____ **NOTE** _____

The word "END" is displayed on row 36 as a result of the formula entered earlier.

The word "VALUE" which you see displayed at the bottom of your worksheet indicates that the formulas have been copied into these cells, allowing you to later add more values as desired. Should any more rows be needed, you will have to copy the formulas down as many columns and rows as needed.

Now that you have entered all your values and formulas, and named them, your worksheet is complete and should look like Figure 1.

Now that your worksheet is complete, it is ready and all you need to do is enter your own set of known values.

_____ **NOTE** _____

Never enter values into cells containing formulas, or the formulas will be erased.

Now proceed with Figure 2.

FINDING THE UNKNOWN PRINCIPAL FROM A KNOWN PAYMENT (Figure 2)

USE THE FOLLOWING STEP-BY-STEP DIRECTIONS FOR FINDING THE UNKNOWN PRINCIPAL, as illustrated in Figure 2.

Your worksheet has already been set up with labels and formulas entered.

First you will blank out the Principal Known value, in column 2, to the right of PV.

Place your cursor on R2C2 and type:

B	starts BLANK command
RETURN	executes the command

Now you may enter your own Payment Known value, in column 2, to the right of CP.

We have used a Payment Known value of $200, for purposes of demonstration.

```
             1              2        3        4        5        6
 1 Payment Known  = CP      200
 2 Principal Known = PV
 3 Interest       = I       0.14
 4 Comp Period/Yr = m       12
 5 # Payments/Yr  = k       12
 6 Total Payments = g       10
 7                      ==========
 8 Part 1,Formula 1=One      1
 9 Payment Unk   = cpun    0.00
10 Principal Unk = pvun  1877.44
11
12        Term          Interest Principal Principal Interest Principal
13                      Payment  Payment   Owing    Pd.ToDate Pd.ToDate
14 --------------------------------------------------------------------
15                                          1877.44
16                 1    21.90    178.10    1699.34   21.90    178.10
17                 2    19.83    180.17    1519.16   41.73    358.27
18                 3    17.72    182.28    1336.89   59.45    540.55
19                 4    15.60    184.40    1152.49   75.05    724.95
20                 5    13.45    186.55     965.93   88.50    911.50
21                 6    11.27    188.73     777.20   99.76   1100.24
22                 7     9.07    190.93     586.27  108.83   1291.17
23                 8     6.84    193.16     393.11  115.67   1484.33
24                 9     4.59    195.41     197.69  120.26   1679.74
25                10     2.31    197.69       0.00  122.56   1877.44
26 END                 #VALUE!  #VALUE!   #VALUE!  #VALUE!  #VALUE!
27      #VALUE!        #VALUE!  #VALUE!   #VALUE!  #VALUE!  #VALUE!
28      #VALUE!        #VALUE!  #VALUE!   #VALUE!  #VALUE!  #VALUE!
29      #VALUE!        #VALUE!  #VALUE!   #VALUE!  #VALUE!  #VALUE!
30      #VALUE!        #VALUE!  #VALUE!   #VALUE!  #VALUE!  #VALUE!
31      #VALUE!        #VALUE!  #VALUE!   #VALUE!  #VALUE!  #VALUE!
32      #VALUE!        #VALUE!  #VALUE!   #VALUE!  #VALUE!  #VALUE!
33      #VALUE!        #VALUE!  #VALUE!   #VALUE!  #VALUE!  #VALUE!
34      #VALUE!        #VALUE!  #VALUE!   #VALUE!  #VALUE!  #VALUE!
35      #VALUE!        #VALUE!  #VALUE!   #VALUE!  #VALUE!  #VALUE!
36      #VALUE!        #VALUE!  #VALUE!   #VALUE!  #VALUE!  #VALUE!
37      #VALUE!        #VALUE!  #VALUE!   #VALUE!  #VALUE!  #VALUE!
```

Figure 2

Finding the Unknown Principal From a Known Payment

You can also change the other values, i.e.:

The interest (to the right of I),

The number of compounding periods per year (to the right of m),

The number of payments per year (to the right of k), and

The total payments (to the right of g).

We have changed the Interest Rate (to the right of I) to 14%, and changed the Total Payments (to the right of g) to 10 payments, for purposes of demonstration.

If you use the same values as we have shown in Figure 2, your worksheet should like like Figure 2 (Finding the Unknown Principal from a Known Payment).

```
_____ NOTE _____
|                                                          |
|  Never enter values into cells containing formulas, or the formulas  |
|  will be erased.                                         |
|                                                          |
```

SAVING YOUR WORKSHEET

Now save your worksheet for future use, so that the next time you wish to figure this computation all you will need to do is enter in your new known values, and you will not need to retype in the labels or enter the formula.

To save your worksheet, place a formatted data diskette in Drive A.

With your cursor on any location, type:

T	starts TRANSFER command
S	selects Save option

Type in name of file.

RETURN	executes the command

PRINTING YOUR WORKSHEET

To print your worksheet, type:

P	starts PRINT command
P	selects Print option and prints

```
_____ NOTE _____
|                                                                       |
|  If you wish to set an Epson printer to compressed font, type:        |
|                                                                       |
|  P          starts PRINT command                                      |
|                                                                       |
|  O          selects Options option                                    |
|                                                                       |
|  TAB        moves cursor to Setup:                                    |
|                                                                       |
|  ˆO         sets Epson printer to compressed font                     |
|             Note: type **letter** O                                   |
|                                                                       |
|  RETURN     prepares for another option selection                     |
|                                                                       |
|  P          selects Print option, and prints                          |
|                                                                       |
```

LOADING YOUR WORKSHEET BACK INTO MULTIPLAN

At a later date, when you need to use the worksheet to do further computations, just load your worksheet back into memory.

To do this, you must first clear memory if there is anything in it. To clear the memory,

Leave your cursor on any location and type:

T	starts TRANSFER command
C	selects Clear option
Y	Yes, to confirm

Now you are ready to load the worksheet into the memory. To do this,

Place the data diskette from which you wish to load into Drive A.

Leave your cursor on any location and type:

T	starts TRANSFER command
L	selects Load option

Type in the name of the file you wish to load.

RETURN	executes the command

_____ **NOTE** _____

Remember, never enter values into cells containing formulas, or the formulas will be erased.

CHAPTER TWO

FINANCING AND PURCHASING A HOME

DESCRIPTION

When considering the purchasing and financing of a home, several factors needs to be considered: The minimum loan payment and maximum loan payment (min. loan payment plus tax and insurance, if applicable), the amount of the loan, the total purchase price and the down payment required.

In determining these factors, it will be necessary to know the buyer's gross monthly income, and what percent of his gross income the lending institution will allow him to apply to the monthly mortgage payment. It is necessary to also determine the annual interest rate, the number of compounding periods per year, the term (years) of the loan, the percent of down payment and the percent of the tax and insurance required.

EXAMPLE

A prospective buyer of a home has a monthly income of $2700 and the bank requires that he apply 25% of that to his monthly mortgage payment. The interest rate is 12%, the number of compounding periods is 12, and the term is 30 years. The bank also requires that a down payment of 15% be applied. The tax and insurance is 3%.

The buyer needs to know what his minimum loan payment, and also what his maximum loan payment would be. He also wants to know how large a loan amount he can afford, which will determine how much he can pay for a house (purchase price), and how much he would have to apply as a down payment on the house.

SETTING UP YOUR WORKSHEET - ENTERING LABELS

USE THE FOLLOWING STEP-BY-STEP DIRECTIONS FOR ENTERING THE LABELS IN FIGURE 1:

```
              1           2           3
    1 Gross Income %    =GI        0.25
    2 Monthly Income    =MI        2700
    3 Interest Rate     = I        0.12
    4 No.Comp.Periods   =CP         12
    5 Term              = T         30
    6 Down Payment %    =DP        0.15
    7 Tax & Insurance %=TI         0.3
    8                         ==========
    9 Min.Loan Payment          519.23 ← (GI*MI)*(1/(1+TI))
   10 Max.Loan Payment             675 ← MIN*(1+TI)
   11 Loan Amount             50478.75 ← MIN*((((1-(1+(I/CP))^-(T*CP))/(I/CP)))
   12 Purchase Price          59386.76 ← (1/(1-DP))*LOAN
   13 Down Payment             8908.01 ← PP-LOAN
```

Figure 1

For typing in labels which are longer than the width of the cell, utilize Multiplan's Format/Continous option, which allows you to connect adjacent cells. To do this,

Place your cursor on R1C1 and type:

F	starts FORMAT command
C	selects Cells option and displays R1C1
:	colon - indicates from-to
R13C2	last cell to format
TAB TAB	moves cursor to Format code:
C	selects Continuous option
RETURN	executes the command

NOTE

Before typing in labels, you must first type:

A   starts ALPHA command which prepares the
                               cell for labeling information

Then type in the label.

[RETURN]   enters the label

To enter the double-dashed line in row 8,

Place your cursor on R8 C3 and type:

A   starts ALPHA command

= = = = = = = = = =   10 equal signs (=)

[RETURN]   enters the double-dashed line

After you have entered all the labels and the double-dashed line, you will begin entering the known values and naming their locations.

ENTERING AND NAMING VALUES

USING THE FOLLOWING STEP-BY-STEP DIRECTIONS FOR ENTERING AND NAMING THE KNOWN VALUES:

NOTE

Naming of cells or groups of cells where values or formulas are placed is only done to make it easier to describe the cells' locations when used in formulas. If you don't name the cells, you can type in the address or point to the cell for cell identification.

Once a cell or group of cells is named, the name remains, regardless of any labels, values or formulas that may be entered into that location.

In this exercise, we have taken the option of naming some of our cells in order to make the construction of the formula(s) easier to understand.

The first value to enter, in column 3, to the right of GI, is the percent of gross income which the bank will allow you to allocate toward your monthly payment (25% of gross income).

Place your cursor on R1C3 and type:

0.25	% of gross income bank allows toward monthly payment
RETURN	enters the value

Now you will name the cell into which you have just entered the value.

Leave your cursor on R1C3 and type:

N	starts NAME command
GI	name given to cell
RETURN	executes the command

The second value in column 3, to the right of MI, should represent your total family income.

Place your cursor on R2C3 and type:

2700	total monthly family income
RETURN	enters the value

Now you will name the cell into which you have just entered the value.

Leave your cursor on R2C3 and type:

N	starts NAME command
MI	name given to cell
RETURN	executes the command

The third value in column 3, to the right of I, represents the annual interest rate being charged by the bank for the loan.

Place your cursor on R3C3 and type:

0.12	annual interest rate
RETURN	enters the value

Now you will name the cell into which you have just entered the value.

Leave your cursor on R3C3 and type:

N	starts NAME command
I	name given to cell
RETURN	executes the command

The fourth value in column 3, to the right of CP, is the number of compounding period per year. In this case the loan is compounded monthly (12). This value is used to convert the interest rate and the term per compounding periods.

Place your cursor on R4C3 and type:

12   number of compounding periods per year.

RETURN   enters the value

Now you will name the cell into which you have just entered the formula.

Leave your cursor on R4C3 and type:

N   starts NAME command

CP   name given to cell

RETURN   executives the command

The fifth value in column 3, to the right of T, is the term of the loan in years.

Place your cursor on R5C3 and type:

30   term of loan (years)

RETURN   enters the value

Now you will name the cell into which you have just entered the value.

Leave your cursor on R5C3 and type:

N   starts NAME command

T   name given to cell

RETURN   executes the command

The sixth value in column 3, to the right of DP, is the percent of down payment required by the bank.

Place your cursor on R6C3 and type:

0.15   % of down payment required

RETURN   enters the value

Now you will name the cell into which you have just entered the value.

Leave your cursor on R6C3 and type:

N   starts NAME command

DP	name given to cell

RETURN	executes the command

The seventh value in column 3, to the right of TI, is the percent of tax and insurance to be added to the minimum loan payment.

Place your cursor and R7C3 and type:

0.3	% of tax and insurance

RETURN	enters the value

Now you will name the cell into which you have just entered the value.

Leave your cursor on R7C3 and type:

N	starts NAME command
TI	name given to cell

RETURN	enters the value

Now that you have entered all the known values, you will enter the formulas.

ENTERING FORMULAS

USE THE FOLLOWING STEP-BY-STEP DIRECTIONS FOR ENTERING THE FORMULAS WHICH WILL CALCULATE THE UNKNOWN VALUES, and name them if the values generated by them are needed in another formula.

Formula one, in column 3, underneath the double-dashed line, to the right of Min. Loan Payment, calculates the minimum loan payment, using the following information: percent of gross income, monthly gross income and the tax and insurance percentage.

Place your cursor on R9C3 and type:

(GI * M I) * (1 / (1 + T I))	formula

RETURN	enters the formula

You now need to format the cell so that it will be displayed with two decimal places. To do this:

Leave your cursor on R9C3 and type:

F	starts FORMAT command
C	selects Cells option and displays R9C3

TAB TAB	moves cursor to Format Code

F	selects Fixed option
TAB	moves cursor to # of decimals:
2	number of decimal places
RETURN	executes the command

Now you will name the cell into which you have just entered the formula.

Leave your cursor on R9C3 and type:

N	starts NAME command
MIN	name given to cell
RETURN	executies the command

Formula two in column 3, to the right of Max. Loan Payment, calculates the maximum loan payment, which is the minimum loan payment plus tax and insurance.

Place your cursor on R10C3 and type:

V	starts VALUE command
MIN * (1 + T I)	formula
RETURN	enters the formula

Formula three in column 3, to the right of Loan Amount, calculates the loan amount.

Place your cursor on R11C3 and type:

V	starts VALUE command
MIN * (((1 — (1 + (I / C P))^ — (T * C P)) / (I / C P)))	formula
RETURN	enters the formulas

You now need to format the cell so that it will be displayed with two decimal places. To do this,

Leave your cursor on R11C3 and type:

F	starts FORMAT command
C	selects Cells option and displays R11C3
TAB TAB	moves cursor to Format Code:
F	selects Fixed option
TAB	moves cursor # of decimals:

2	number of decimal places
RETURN	executes the command

Now you will name the cell into which you have just entered the formula.

Leave your cursor on R11C3 and type:

N	starts NAME command
LOAN	name given to cell
RETURN	executes the command

Formula four in column 3, to the right of Purchase Price, calculates the total purchase price.

Place your cursor on R12C3 and type:

(1 / (1 — D P)) * LOAN	formula
RETURN	enters the formula

You now need to format the cell so that it will be displayed with two decimal places. To do this,

Leave your cursor on R12C3 and type:

F	starts FORMAT command
C	selects Cells option and displays R12C3
TAB TAB	moves cursor to Format Code:
F	selects Fixed option
TAB	moves cursor # of decimals:
2	number of decimal places
RETURN	executes the command

Now you will name the cell into which you have just entered the formula.

Leave your cursor on R12C3 and type:

N	starts NAME command
PP	name given to cell
RETURN	executes the command

Formula five in column 3, to the right of Down Payment, determines the amount of down payment.

Place your cursor on R13C3 and type:

V	starts VALUE command
PP-LOAN	formula
RETURN	enters the formula

You now need to format the cell so that it will be displayed with two decimal places. To do this,

Leave your cursor on R13C3 and type:

F	starts FORMAT command
C	selects Cells option and displays R13C3
TAB TAB	moves cursor to Format Code:
F	selects Fixed option
TAB	moves cursor to # of decimals:
2	number of decimal places
RETURN	executes the command

Now that you have entered all your values and formulas, and named them, your worksheet is complete and should look like Figure 1.

Now that your worksheet is complete, it is ready and all you need to do is enter your own set of known values.

NOTE

Never enter values into cells containing formulas, or the formulas will be erased.

SAVING YOUR WORKSHEET

Now save your worksheet for future use, so that the next time you wish to figure this computation all you will need to do is enter in your new known values, and you will not need to retype in the labels or enter the formula.

To save your worksheet, place a formatted data diskette in Drive A.

With your cursor on any location, type:

T	starts TRANSFER command

S	selects Save option

Type in name of file.

RETURN	executes the command

PRINTING YOUR WORKSHEET

To print your worksheet, type:

P	starts PRINT command
P	selects Print option and prints

NOTE

If you wish to set an Epson printer to compressed font, type:

P	starts PRINT command
O	selects Options option
TAB	moves cursor to Setup:
^O	sets Epson printer to compressed font Note: type **letter** O
RETURN	prepares for another option selection
P	selects Print option, and prints

LOADING YOUR WORKSHEET BACK INTO MULTIPLAN

At a later date, when you need to use the worksheet to do further computations, just load your worksheet back into memory.

To do this, you must first clear memory if there is anything in it. To clear the memory,

Leave your cursor on any location and type:

T	starts TRANSFER command
C	selects Clear option
Y	Yes, to confirm

Now you are ready to load the worksheet into the memory. To do this,

Place the data diskette from which you wish to load into Drive A.

Leave your cursor on any location and type:

T	starts TRANSFER command

L   selects Load option

Type in the name of the file you wish to load.

[RETURN]   executes the command

———————— NOTE ————————

> Remember, never enter values into cells containing formulas, or the formulas will be erased.

CHAPTER THREE

PRESENT VALUE WITH CONTINUOUS COMPOUNDING

DESCRIPTION

Continuous compounding means that the interest is computed continuously during the period. To determine the present value of a business, the revenue generated each year must be considered, along with the discount rate and the method of computing it.

EXAMPLE

Aroma Coffee Corporation has coffee vending machines disbursed widely throughout the city. Each machine generates $6,000 in revenue every year. The discount rate is 12% annual with continuous compounding.

What would the present value be of four years' operation of each machine (before taxes, insurance, maintenance expenses, etc.)?

SETTING UP YOUR WORKSHEET - ENTERING LABELS

USE THE FOLLOWING STEP-BY-STEP DIRECTIONS FOR ENTERING THE LABELS IN FIGURE 1:

_____ **NOTE** _____

Before typing in labels, you must first type:

A   starts ALPHA command which prepares the
                cell for labeling information

Then type in the label.

RETURN   enters label

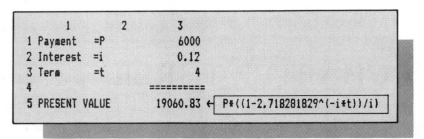

```
          1           2          3
1 Payment     =P          6000
2 Interest    =i          0.12
3 Term        =t          4
4                      ==========
5 PRESENT VALUE        19060.83  ← P*((1-2.718281829^(-i*t))/i)
```

Figure 1

To enter the double-dashed line in row 4,

Place your cursor on R4C3 and type:

A	starts ALPHA command
= = = = = = = = = =	10 equal signs (=)
RETURN	executes the command

After you have entered all the labels and the double-dashed line, you will begin entering the known values and naming their locations.

ENTERING AND NAMING VALUES

USE THE FOLLOWING STEP-BY-STEP DIRECTIONS FOR ENTERING AND NAMING THE KNOWN VALUES:

___ **NOTE** ___

Naming of cells or groups of cells where values or formulas are placed is only done to make it easier to describe the cells' locations when used in formulas. If you don't name the cells, you can type in the address or point to the cell for cell identification.

Once a cell or a group of cells is named, the name remains, regardless of any labels, values or formulas that may be entered into that location.

In this exercise, we have taken the option of naming some of our cells in order to make the construction of the formula(s) easier to understand.

The first value to enter, in column 3, to the right of P, is the Payment.

Place your cursor on R1C3 and type:

6000	payment
RETURN	enters the value

Now you will name the cell into which you have just entered the value.

Leave your cursor on R1C3 and type:

N   starts NAME command

P   name given to cell

| RETURN | executes the command

The second value, in column 3, to the right of i, is the Interest Rate.

Place your cursor on R2C3 and type:

0.12   interest rate

| RETURN | enters the value

Now you will name the cell into which you have just entered the value.

Leave your cursor on R2C3 and type:

N   starts NAME command

i   name given to cell

| RETURN | executes the command

The third value in column 3, to the right of t, is the Term.

Place your cursor on R3C3 and type:

4   term

| RETURN | enters the value

Now you will name the cell into which you have just entered the value.

Leave your cursor on R3C3 and type:

N   starts NAME command

t   name given to cell

| RETURN | executes the command

Now that you have entered all the known values, you will enter the formula.

ENTERING THE FORMULA

USE THE FOLLOWING STEP-BY-STEP DIRECTIONS FOR ENTERING THE FORMULA
WHICH WILL CALCULATE THE UNKNOWN VALUE:

Place your cursor on R5C3 and type:

V	starts VALUE command
P*((1-2.718281829^(-i*t))/i)	formula
RETURN	enters the formula

Now that you have entered all your values and formulas, and named them, your worksheet is complete and should look like Figure 1.

Now that your worksheet is complete, it is ready and all you need to do is enter your own set of known values.

─────────── **NOTE** ───────────

Never enter values into cells containing formulas, or the formulas will be erased.

SAVING YOUR WORKSHEET

Now save your worksheet for future use, so that the next time you wish to figure this computation all you will need to do is enter in your new known values, and you will not need to retype in the labels or enter the formula.

To save your worksheet, place a formatted data diskette in Drive A.

With your cursor on any location, type:

T	starts TRANSFER command
S	selects Save option

Type in name of file.

RETURN	executes the command

PRINTING YOUR WORKSHEET

To print your worksheet, type:

P	starts PRINT command
P	selects Print option and prints

_____ **NOTE** _____

If you wish to set an Epson printer to compressed font, type:

P	starts PRINT command
O	selects Options option
TAB	moves cursor to Setup:
ˆO	sets Epson printer to compressed font Note: type **letter** O
RETURN	prepares for another option selection
P	selects Print option, and prints

LOADING YOUR WORKSHEET BACK INTO MULTIPLAN

At a later date, when you need to use the worksheet to do further computations, just load your worksheet back into memory.

To do this, you must first clear memory if there is anything in it. To clear the memory,

Leave your cursor on any location and type:

T	starts TRANSFER command
C	selects Clear option
Y	Yes, to confirm

Now you are ready to load the worksheet into the memory. To do this,

Place the data diskette from which you wish to load into Drive A.

Leave your cursor on any location and type:

T	starts TRANSFER command
L	selects Load option

Type in the name of the file you wish to load.

RETURN	executes the command

_____ **NOTE** _____

Remember, never enter values into cells containing formulas, or the formulas will be erased.

CHAPTER FOUR

FUTURE VALUE WITH CONTINUOUS COMPOUNDING

DESCRIPTION

Continuous compounding means that the interest is computed continuously during the period. To determine the future value of a series of yearly payments which are deposited in an account for five years, it is necessary to determine the amount of the yearly payments, the rate of interest, and the method of computing interest.

EXAMPLE

For a five year period, Mr. Abernathy will be able to deposit $1,500 each year into an account. The payments will be compounded continuously at a rate of 6.5% annually.

What will the value of the payments be at the end of five years?

SETTING UP YOUR WORKSHEET - ENTERING LABELS

USE THE FOLLOWING STEP-BY-STEP DIRECTIONS FOR ENTERING THE LABELS IN FIGURE 1:

First you will expand the width of column 1. To do this,

Place your cursor on R1C1 and type:

F	starts FORMAT command
W	selects Width option
12	column width
RETURN	executes the command

```
         1          2
1 Payment    =P     1500
2 Interest   =i     0.065
3 Term Yr.   =t        5
4                  ==========
5 Future Value  8862.25  ← P*((2.718281829^(i*t)-1)/i)
```

Figure 1

NOTE

Before typing in labels, you must first type:

A   starts ALPHA command which prepares the
                       cell for labeling information

Then type in the label.

RETURN   enters label

To enter the double-dashed line in row 4,

Place your cursor on R4C2 and type:

A   starts ALPHA command

= = = = = = = = = =   10 equal signs (=)

RETURN   executes the command

After you have entered all the labels, you will begin entering the known values and naming their locations.

ENTERING AND NAMING VALUES

USE THE FOLLOWING STEP-BY-STEP DIRECTIONS FOR ENTERING AND NAMING THE KNOWN VALUES:

```
_____ NOTE _____

Naming of cells or groups of cells where values or formulas are
placed is only done to make it easier to describe the cells' loca-
tions when used in formulas. If you don't name the cells, you can
type in the address or point to the cell for cell identification.

Once a cell or a group of cells is named, the name remains,
regardless of any labels, values or formulas that may be entered
into that location.

In this exercise, we have taken the option of naming some of our
cells in order to make the construction of the formula(s) easier to
understand.
```

The first value to enter, in column 2, to the right of P, is the Payment.

Place your cursor on R1C2 and type:

1500	yearly payment
RETURN	enters the value

Now you will name the cell into which you have just entered the value.

Leave your cursor on R1C2 and type:

N	starts NAME command
P	name given to cell
RETURN	executes the command

The second value, in column 2, to the right of i, is the Interest Rate.

Place your cursor on R2C2 and type:

0.065	interest rate
RETURN	enters the value

Now you will name the cell into which you have just entered the value.

Leave your cursor on R2C2 and type:

N	starts NAME command
i	name given to cell
RETURN	executes the command

The third value in column 2, to the right of t, is the period over which the payments will be made (Term Yr.).

Place your cursor on R3C2 and type:

5   number of years during which the payments will be made

RETURN   enters the value

Now you will name the cell into which you have just entered the value.

Leave your cursor on R3C2 and type:

N   starts NAME command

t   name given to cell

RETURN   executes the command

Now that you have entered all the known values, you will enter the formula.

ENTERING THE FORMULA

USE THE FOLLOWING STEP-BY-STEP DIRECTIONS FOR ENTERING THE FORMULA WHICH WILL CALCULATE THE UNKNOWN VALUE:

The formula, in column 2, to the right of Future Value, will calculate the future value for an annuity invested in even amounts over a 5 year period, with continuous compounding of interest.

Place your cursor on R5C2 and type:

V   starts VALUE command

P * ((2.718281829 ^ (i * t) - 1) / i)   formula

RETURN   enters the formula

You now need to format the cell so that it will be displayed with two decimal places. To do this,

Leave your cursor on R5C2 and type:

F   starts FORMAT command

C   selects Cells option and displays R5C2

TAB TAB   moves cursor to Format Code:

F   selects Fixed option

TAB   moves cursor to # of decimals:

2	number of decimal palces
RETURN	executes the command

Now that you have entered all your values and formulas, and named them, your worksheet is complete and should look like Figure 1.

Now that your worksheet is complete, it is ready and all you need to do is enter your own set of known values.

_____ NOTE _____

Never enter values into cells containing formulas, or the formulas will be erased.

SAVING YOUR WORKSHEET

Now save your worksheet for future use, so that the next time you wish to figure this computation all you will need to do is enter in your new known values, and you will not need to retype in the labels or enter the formula.

To save your worksheet, place a formatted data diskette in Drive A.

With your cursor on any location, type:

T	starts TRANSFER command
S	selects Save option

Type in name of file.

RETURN	executes the command

PRINTING YOUR WORKSHEET

To print your worksheet, type:

P	starts PRINT command
P	selects Print option and prints

```
_____ NOTE _____

If you wish to set an Epson printer to compressed font, type:

P                    starts PRINT command

O                    selects Options option

[TAB]                moves cursor to Setup:

^O                   sets Epson printer to compressed font
                     Note: type letter O

[RETURN]             prepares for another option selection

P                    selects Print option, and prints
```

LOADING YOUR WORKSHEET BACK INTO MULTIPLAN

At a later date, when you need to use the worksheet to do further computations, just load your worksheet back into memory.

To do this, you must first clear memory if there is anything in it. To clear the memory,

Leave your cursor on any location and type:

T	starts TRANSFER command
C	selects Clear option
Y	Yes, to confirm

Now you are ready to load the worksheet into the memory. To do this,

Place the data diskette from which you wish to load into Drive A.

Leave your cursor on any location and type:

T	starts TRANSFER command
L	selects Load option

Type in the name of the file you wish to load.

[RETURN]	executes the command

```
_____ NOTE _____

Remember, never enter values into cells containing formulas, or
the formulas will be erased.
```

CHAPTER FIVE

FINDING PV FROM FV CONTINUOUS COMPOUNDING

DESCRIPTION

Continuously compounding means that the compounding takes place continuously over the time periods, rather than at the end of each period. In this exercise, you will determine the unknown present value from the known future value. You will use Euler's constant, which is a constant used in computing continuous compounding.

EXAMPLE

Mr. Huber wants to accumulate $10,500 in his savings account at the end of 6 years. The annual rate of interest is 8.5% compounded continuously.

What is the present value of his savings account, i.e., how much money should he deposit now in order to accumulate the $10,500 at the end of 6 years?

SETTING UP YOUR WORKSHEET - ENTERING LABELS

USE THE FOLLOWING STEP-BY-STEP DIRECTIONS FOR ENTERING THE LABELS IN FIGURE 1:

For typing in labels which are longer than the width of the cell, utilize Multiplan's Format/Continuous option, which allows you to connect adjacent cells. To do this,

Place your cursor on R1C1 and type:

F	starts FORMAT command
C	selects Cells option and displays R1C1
:	colon - indicates from-to

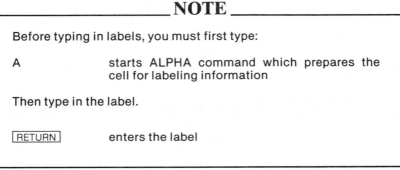

Figure 1

R12C4	last cell to format
TAB TAB	moves cursor to Format code:
C	selects Continuous option
RETURN	executes the command

NOTE

Before typing in labels, you must first type:

A   starts ALPHA command which prepares the cell for labeling information

Then type in the label.

RETURN   enters the label

After you have entered all the labels, you will begin entering the known values and naming their locations.

ENTERING AND NAMING VALUES

USE THE FOLLOWING STEP-BY-STEP DIRECTIONS FOR ENTERING AND NAMING THE KNOWN VALUES:

_____ **NOTE** _____

Naming of cells or groups of cells where values or formulas are placed is only done to make it easier to describe the cells' locations when used in formulas. If you don't name the cells, you can type in the address or point to the cell for cell identification.

Once a cell or a group of cells is named, the name remains, regardless of any labels, values or formulas that may be entered into that location.

In this exercise, we have taken the option of naming some of our cells in order to make the construction of the formula(s) easier to understand.

The first value to enter, in column 5, to the right of FV, is the Future Value. To enter the value,

Place your cursor on R3C5 and type:

10500	future value
RETURN	enters the value

Now name the cell into which you have just entered the value.

Leave your cursor on R3C5 and type:

N	starts NAME command
FV	name given to cell
RETURN	executes the command

The second value, in column 5, to the right of rate, is the Interest Rate Per Time Period (as a decimal).

Place your cursor on R6C5 and type:

0.085	interest rate per time period
RETURN	enters the value

Now name the cell into which you have just entered the value.

Leave your cursor on R6C5 and type:

N	starts NAME command
rate	name given to cell
RETURN	executes the command

The third value, in column 5, to the right of n, is the Time Period.

Place your cursor on R8C5 and type:

6	time period (number of years)
RETURN	enters the value

Now name the cell into which you have just entered the value.

Leave your cursor on R8C5 and type:

N	starts NAME command
n	name given to cell
RETURN	executes the command

The fourth value, in column 5, to the right of e, is Euler's Constant (the constant used in computing continuous compounding).

Place your cursor on R10C5 and type:

2.718281829	Euler's constant
RETURN	enters the value

Now name the cell into which you have just entered the value.

Leave your cursor on R10C5 and type:

N	starts NAME command
e	name given to cell
RETURN	executes the command

Now that you have entered all the known values, you will enter the formula.

ENTERING THE FORMULA

USE THE FOLLOWING STEP-BY-STEP DIRECTIONS FOR ENTERING THE FORMULA WHICH WILL CALCULATE THE UNKNOWN VALUE:

Enter the formula in column 5, to the right of PV, which will calculate the Present Value. To do this,

Place your cursor on R12C5 and type:

V	starts VALUE command
FV * (e ^ (- rate * n))	formula
RETURN	enters the formula

You now need to format the cell so that it will be displayed with 2 decimal places. To do this,

Leave your cursor on R12C5 and type:

F	starts FORMAT command
C	selects Cells option and displays R12C5
TAB TAB	moves cursor to Format Code:
F	selects Fixed option
TAB	moves cursor to # of decimals:
2	number of decimal places
RETURN	executes the command

Now that you have entered all your values and formulas, and named them, your worksheet is complete and should look like Figure 1.

Now that your worksheet is complete, it is ready and all you need to do is enter your own set of known values.

NOTE

Never enter values into cells containing formulas, or the formulas will be erased.

SAVING YOUR WORKSHEET

Now save your worksheet for future use, so that the next time you wish to figure this computation all you will need to do is enter in your new known values, and you will not need to retype in the labels or enter the formula.

To save your worksheet, place a formatted data diskette in Drive A.

With your cursor on any location, type:

T	starts TRANSFER command
S	selects Save option

Type in name of file.

RETURN	executes the command

PRINTING YOUR WORKSHEET

To print your worksheet, type:

P   starts PRINT command

P   selects Print option and prints

NOTE

If you wish to set an Epson printer to compressed font, type:

P   starts PRINT command

O   selects Options option

TAB   moves cursor to Setup:

^O   sets Epson printer to compressed font
                   Note: type **letter** O

RETURN   prepares for another option selection

P   selects Print option, and prints

LOADING YOUR WORKSHEET BACK INTO MULTIPLAN

At a later date, when you need to use the worksheet to do further computations, just load your worksheet back into memory.

To do this, you must first clear memory if there is anything in it. To clear the memory,

Leave your cursor on any location and type:

T   starts TRANSFER command

C   selects Clear option

Y   Yes, to confirm

Now you are ready to load the worksheet into the memory. To do this,

Place the data diskette from which you wish to load into Drive A.

Leave your cursor on any location and type:

T   starts TRANSFER command

L   selects Load option

Type in the name of the file you wish to load.

RETURN   executes the command

CHAPTER SIX

FINDING FV FROM PV CONTINUOUS COMPOUNDING

DESCRIPTION

Continuously compounding means that the compounding takes place continuously over the time periods, rather than at the end of each period. In this exercise, you will determine the unknown future value from the known present value. You will use Euler's constant, which is a constant used in computing continuous compounding.

EXAMPLE

If $5,000 is invested in a savings account at a bank which pays 6% interest, compounded continuously, what will be the future value of the account at the end of a 3-year period?

SETTING UP YOUR WORKSHEET - ENTERING LABELS

USE THE FOLLOWING STEP-BY-STEP DIRECTIONS FOR ENTERING THE LABELS IN FIGURE 1:

For typing in labels which are longer than the width of the cell, utilize Multiplan's Format/Continuous option, which allows you to connect adjacent cells. To do this,

Place your cursor on R1C1 and type:

F	starts FORMAT command
C	selects Cells option and displays R1C1
:	colon - indicates from-to
R12C4	last cell to format

```
           1        2        3        4        5
1              FINDING FV FROM PV CONTINUOUS COMPOUNDING
2
3 Present Value                    =  PV      5000
4
5 Time Period                      =  n         36
6
7 Euler's Constant (2.718281829)   =  e     2.7182818
8
9 Interest Rate Per Time Period
10    As A Decimal                 =  rate    0.005  ←  0.06/12
11
12 Future Value                    =  FV    5986.09  ←  PV*(e^(rate*n))
```

Figure 1

TAB TAB	moves cursor to Format code:
C	selects Continuous option
RETURN	executes the command

NOTE

Before typing in labels, you must first type:

A   starts ALPHA command which prepares the cell for labeling information

Then type in the label.

RETURN   enters the label

After you have entered all the labels, you will begin entering the known values and naming their locations.

ENTERING AND NAMING VALUES

USE THE FOLLOWING STEP-BY-STEP DIRECTIONS FOR ENTERING AND NAMING THE KNOWN VALUES:

NOTE

Naming of cells or groups of cells where values or formulas are placed is only done to make it easier to describe the cells' locations when used in formulas. If you don't name the cells, you can type in the address or point to the cell for cell identification.

Once a cell or a group of cells is named, the name remains, regardless of any labels, values or formulas that may be entered into that location.

In this exercise, we have taken the option of naming some of our cells in order to make the construction of the formula(s) easier to understand.

The first value to enter, in column 5, to the right of PV, is the Present Value.

Place your cursor on R3C5 and type:

5000	present value

RETURN	enters the value

Now name the cell into which you have just entered the value.

Leave your cursor on R3C5 and type:

N	starts NAME command
PV	name given to cell

RETURN	executes the command

The second value, in column 5, to the right of n, is the Time Period.

Place your cursor on R5C5 and type:

36	time period (months)

RETURN	enters the value

Now name the cell into which you have just entered the value.

Leave your cursor on R5C5 and type:

N	starts NAME command
n	name given to cell

RETURN	executes the command

The third value, in column 5, to the right of e, is Euler's Constant, the constant used in computing continuous compounding.

Place your cursor on R7C5 and type:

2.718281829	Euler's constant
RETURN	enters the value

Now name the cell into which you have just entered the value.

Leave your cursor on R7C5 and type:

N	starts NAME command
e	name given to cell
RETURN	executes the command

Now that you have entered all the known values, you will enter the formula.

ENTERING THE FORMULAS

USE THE FOLLOWING STEP-BY-STEP DIRECTIONS FOR ENTERING THE FORMULAS WHICH WILL CALCULATE THE UNKNOWN VALUES, and name them if the values generated by them are needed in another formula.

Formula one, in column 5, to the right of rate, computes the Interest Rate Per Time Period As A Decimal.

Place your cursor on R10C5 and type:

0.06/12	formula for interest rate
RETURN	enters the formula

Now name the cell into which you have just entered the formula.

Leave your cursor on R10C5 and type:

N	starts NAME command
rate	name given to cell
RETURN	executes the command

Formula two, in column 5, to the right of FV, computes the Future Value.

Place your cursor on R12C5 and type:

V	starts VALUE command
PV * (e $^{\wedge}$ (rate * n))	formula
RETURN	enters the formula

You now need to format the cell so that it will be displayed with two decimal places. To do this,

Leave your cursor on R12C5 and type:

F	starts FORMAT command
C	selects Cells option and displays R12C5
TAB TAB	moves cursor to Format Code:
F	selects Fixed option
TAB	moves cursor to # of decimals:
2	number of decimal places
RETURN	executes the command

Now that you have entered all your values and formulas, and named them, your worksheet is complete and should look like Figure 1.

Now that your worksheet is complete, it is ready and all you need to do is enter your own set of known values.

___**NOTE**___

Never enter values into cells containing formulas, or the formulas will be erased.

SAVING YOUR WORKSHEET

Now save your worksheet for future use, so that the next time you wish to figure this computation all you will need to do is enter in your new known values, and you will not need to retype in the labels or enter the formula.

To save your worksheet, place a formatted data diskette in Drive A.

With your cursor on any location, type:

T	starts TRANSFER command
S	selects Save option

Type in name of file.

RETURN	executes the command

PRINTING YOUR WORKSHEET

To print your worksheet, type:

P   starts PRINT command

P   selects Print option and prints

___ NOTE ___

If you wish to set an Epson printer to compressed font, type:

P   starts PRINT command

O   selects Options option

[TAB]   moves cursor to Setup:

^O   sets Epson printer to compressed font
                     Note: type **letter** O

[RETURN]   prepares for another option selection

P   selects Print option, and prints

LOADING YOUR WORKSHEET BACK INTO MULTIPLAN

At a later date, when you need to use the worksheet to do further computations, just load your worksheet back into memory.

To do this, you must first clear memory if there is anything in it. To clear the memory,

Leave your cursor on any location and type:

T   starts TRANSFER command

C   selects Clear option

Y   Yes, to confirm

Now you are ready to load the worksheet into the memory. To do this,

Place the data diskette from which you wish to load into Drive A.

Leave your cursor on any location and type:

T   starts TRANSFER command

L   selects Load option

Type in the name of the file you wish to load.

[RETURN]   executes the command

_____ **NOTE** _____

Remember, never enter values into cells containing formulas, or
the formulas will be erased.

CHAPTER SEVEN

GENERAL ANNUITY DUE (Solving for Cash Payment - Present Value)

DESCRIPTION

An annuity due involves payments made at the beginning of each payment period. Most leases are considered an annuity due.

EXAMPLE

You own farmland which has a present value of $100,000 and want to lease it to a soy bean grower for 25 years. You want to earn an annual return of 18% annual interest, compounded quarterly. The soy bean grower will make his lease payments annually at the beginning of each year.

What will be the amount of the annual payments to you?

SETTING UP YOUR WORKSHEET — ENTERING LABELS

USE THE FOLLOWING STEP-BY-STEP DIRECTIONS FOR ENTERING THE LABELS IN FIGURE 1:

First you will need to expand column 1 to allow for the labels.

Place your cursor on column 1 and type:

F   starts FORMAT command

W   selects Width option

```
               1            2
1 Present Value        =PV    100000
2 Number Of Years      =ny        25
3 Annual Return %      =ar      0.18
4 Compounding Per Yr   =cp         4
5 Payment Per Year     =pp         1
6                             ==========
7 Part 1,Formula 1=One     16143.866  ← (1-((1+(ar/cp))^-(cp/pp)))*PV
8 Payment for PV           16344.19   ← One/(ar/cp)/((1-((1+(ar/cp))^-(cp*ny*pp/pp)))/(ar/cp))
```

Figure 1

25   width of column

RETURN   executes the command

NOTE

Before typing in labels, you must first type:

A   starts ALPHA command which prepares the
                      cell for labeling information

Then type in the label.

RETURN   enters label

Now enter the double-dashed line in row 6. To do this,

Place your cursor on R6C2 and type:

A   starts ALPHA command

= = = = = = = = = =   10 equal signs (=)

RETURN   executes the command

After you have entered all the labels, and the double-dashed line, you will begin entering the known
values and naming their locations.

ENTERING AND NAMING VALUES

NOTE

Naming of cells or groups of cells where values or formulas are placed is only done to make it easier to describe the cells' locations when used in formulas. If you don't name the cells, you can type in the address or point to the cell for cell identification.

Once a cell or group of cells is named, the name remains, regardless of any labels, values or formulas that may be entered into that location.

In this exercise, we have taken the option of naming some of our cells in order to make the construction of the formula(s) easier to understand.

The first value to enter, in column 2, to the right of PV, is the Present Value.

Place your cursor on R1C2 and type:

100000	present value
[RETURN]	enters the value

Now you will name the cell into which you have just entered the value.

Leave your cursor on R1C2 and type:

N	starts NAME command
PV	name given to cell
[RETURN]	executes the command

The second value, in column 2, to the right of ny, is the Number of Years.

Place your cursor on R2C2 and type:

25	number of years
[RETURN]	enters the value

Now you will name the cell into which you have just entered the value.

Leave your cursor on R2C2 and type:

N	starts NAME command
ny	name given to cell
[RETURN]	executes the command

The third value, in column 2, to the right of ar, is the Annual Return Percentage.

Place your cursor on R3C2 and type:

0.18	annual return percent
RETURN	enters the value

Now you will name the cell into which you have just entered the value.

Leave your cursor on R3C2 and type:

N	starts NAME command
ar	name given to cell
RETURN	executes the command

The fourth value, in column 2, to the right of cp, is the number of compounding periods per year.

Place your cursor on R4C2 and type:

4	number of compounding periods per year
RETURN	enters the value

Now you will name the cell into which you have just entered the value.

Leave your cursor on R4C2 and type:

N	starts NAME command
cp	name given to cell
RETURN	executes the command

The fifth value, in column 2, to the right of pp, is the Payment Per Year.

Place your cursor on R5C2 and type:

1	payment per year
RETURN	enters the value

Now you will name the cell into which you have just entered the value.

Leave your cursor on on R5C2 and type:

N	starts NAME command
pp	name given to cell
RETURN	executes the command

Now that you have entered all the known values, you will enter the formula.

ENTERING THE FORMULA

USE THE FOLLOWING STEP-BY-STEP DIRECTIONS FOR ENTERING THE FORMULA WHICH WILL CALCULATE THE UNKNOWN VALUE:

_____ **NOTE** _____

> Multiplan will not accept the formula in its entirety, because it has too many words. As a result, we have to break the formula into two parts. Therefore, the procedure for entering the formula will be different from the usual procedure.
>
> Follow the step-by-step directions carefully for entering the formula.

The formula, in column 2, to the right of Payment for PV, calculates the present value payment.

Enter the first part of the formula, in column 2, immediately underneath the double-dashed line, to the right of One. To do this,

Place your cursor on R7C2 and type:

$(1 - ((1 + (ar/cp))^{\hat{}} - (cp/pp))) * PV$ first part of the formula

RETURN   enters the first part of the formula

Now you will name the first part of the formula. To do this,

Leave your cursor on R7C2 and type:

N   starts NAME command

One   name given to cell

RETURN   executes the command

Now you will be able to enter the formula, in column 2, to the right of Payment for PV, which will calculate the Present Value payment. To do this,

Place your cursor on R8C2 and type:

V   starts VALUE command

One   part one of formula

/   divides

$(ar/cp)/((1 - ((1 + (ar/cp))^{\hat{}} - (cp*ny*pp/pp)))/(ar/cp))$ second part of formula

RETURN   enters the formula

Now that you have entered all your values and the formula, and named them, your worksheet is complete and should look like Figure 1.

Now that your worksheet is complete, it is ready and all you need to do is enter your own set of known values.

_____ **NOTE** _____

> Never enter values into cells containing formulas, or the formulas
> will be erased.

SAVING YOUR WORKSHEET

Now save your worksheet for future use, so that the next time you wish to figure this computation all you will need to do is enter in your new known values, and you will not need to retype in the labels or enter the formula.

To save your worksheet, place a formatted data diskette in Drive A.

With your cursor on any location, type:

T	starts TRANSFER command
S	selects Save option

Type in name of file.

RETURN	executes the command

PRINTING YOUR WORKSHEET

To print your worksheet, type:

P	starts PRINT command
P	selects Print option and prints

_____ **NOTE** _____

If you wish to set an Epson printer to compressed font, type:	
P	starts PRINT command
O	selects Options option
TAB	moves cursor to Setup:
O	sets Epson printer to compressed font Note: type **letter** O
RETURN	prepares for another option selection
P	selects Print option, and prints

LOADING YOUR WORKSHEET BACK INTO MULTIPLAN

At a later date, when you need to use the worksheet to do further computations, just load your worksheet back into memory.

To do this, you must first clear memory if there is anything in it. To clear the memory,

Leave your cursor on any location and type:

T	starts TRANSFER command
C	selects Clear option
Y	Yes, to confirm

Now you are ready to load the worksheet into the memory. To do this,

Place the data diskette from which you wish to load into Drive A.

Leave your cursor on any location and type:

T	starts TRANSFER command
L	selects Load option

Type in the name of the file you wish to load.

RETURN	executes the command

_____ **NOTE** _____

Remember, never enter values into cells containing formulas, or the formulas will be erased.

CHAPTER EIGHT

GENERAL ANNUITY DUE
Solving for
Weekly Cash Payment

DESCRIPTION

To calculate the weekly cash payment required as a deposit at the beginning of each week, in order to accumulate a specified amount of money in a savings account at the end of a 3-year period, the annual interest percentage the bank pays, and the number of compounding periods in a year must be considered.

EXAMPLE

Your goal is to accumulate $5000 in your savings account at the end of three years. You plan on making weekly deposits every Monday for the three-year period. Your savings account draws 6.5% annual interest and is compounded monthly.

How much should your weekly deposit be in order to reach your goal of accumulating $5000 at the end of three years?

SETTING UP YOUR WORKSHEET - ENTERING LABELS

USE THE FOLLOWING STEP-BY-STEP DIRECTIONS FOR ENTERING THE LABELS IN FIGURE 1.

First you will need to expand column 1 to allow for the labels.

Place your cursor on column 1 and type:

F   starts FORMAT command

W   selects Width option

```
                    1              2
1 Future Value          =FV      5000
2 Number Of Years       =ny         3
3 Annual Return Int.%   =ar     0.065
4 Compounding Periods/Yr=cp        12
5 No. Payments Per Year =pp        52
6                                ==========
7 Part 1 of formula=One    6.2292502  ← (FV*(1-((1+(ar/cp))^-(cp/pp))))
8 ANSWER: Wkly Cash Payment  29.02  ← One/(ar/cp)/(((((1+(ar/cp))^(cp*ny*pp/pp))-1)/(ar/cp))
```

Figure 1

25   width of column

RETURN   executes the command

_____ **NOTE** _____

Before typing in labels, you must first type:

A   starts ALPHA command which prepares the
                 cell for labeling information

Then type in the label.

RETURN   enters label

After you have entered all your labels, you will enter the double dashed line in row 6. To do this,

Place your cursor on R6C2 and type:

A   starts ALPHA command

= = = = = = = = = =   10 equal signs (=)

RETURN   executes the command

After you have entered all the labels, and the double-dashed line, you will begin entering the known values and naming their locations.

NOTE

Naming of cells or groups of cells where values or formulas are placed is only done to make it easier to describe the cells' locations when used in formulas. If you don't name the cells, you can type in the address or point to the cell for cell identification.

Once a cell or group of cells is named, the name remains, regardless of any labels, values or formulas that may be entered into that location.

In this exercise, we have taken the option of naming some of our cells in order to make the construction of the formula(s) easier to understand.

The first value to enter, in column 2, to the right of FV, is the Future Value (the amount you would like to accumulate after 3 years).

Place your cursor on R1C2 and type:

5000	future value
RETURN	enters the value

Now you will name the cell into which you have just entered the value.

Leave your cursor on R1C2 and type:

N	starts NAME command
FV	name given to cell
RETURN	executes the command

The second value, in column 2, to the right of ny, is the number of years you will be making the payments.

Place your cursor on R2C2 and type:

3	number of years
RETURN	enters the value

Now you will name the cell into which you have just entered the value.

Leave your cursor on R2C2 and type:

N	starts NAME command
ny	name given to cell
RETURN	executes the command

The third value, in column 2, to the right of ar, is the Annual Return Percent.

Place your cursor on R3C2 and type:

0.065	annual return percent

RETURN	enters the value

Now you will name the cell into which you have just entered the value.

Leave your cursor on R3C2 and type:

N	starts NAME command
ar	name given to cell

RETURN	executes the command

The fourth value, in column 2, to the right of cp, is the number of compounding periods per year.

Place your cursor on R4C2 and type:

12	number of compounding periods per year

RETURN	enters the value

Now you will name the cell into which you have just entered the value.

Leave your cursor on R4C2 and type:

N	starts NAME command
cp	name given to cell

RETURN	executes the command

The fifth value, in column 2, to the right of pp, is the number of payments you will be making each year.

Place your cursor on R5C2 and type:

52	payments per year

RETURN	enters the value

Now you will name the cell into which you have just entered the value.

Leave your cursor on R5C2 and type:

N	starts NAME command
PP	name given to cell

RETURN	executes the command

Now that you have entered all the known values, you will enter the formula.

ENTERING THE FORMULA

USE THE FOLLOWING STEP-BY-STEP DIRECTIONS FOR ENTERING THE FORMULA WHICH WILL CALCULATE THE UNKNOWN VALUE.

NOTE

Multiplan will not accept the formula in its entirety, because it has too many words. As a result, we have to break the formula into two parts. Therefore, the procedure for entering the formula will be different from the usual procedure.

Follow the step-by-step directions carefully for entering the formula.

The formula in column 2, to the right of Weekly Cash Payment, will calculate the weekly cash payment.

Enter the first part of the formula, in column 2, immediately underneath the double-dashed line, to the right of One. To do this,

Place your cursor on R7C2 and type:

$(FV * (1 - ((1 + (ar/cp))^- (cp/pp))))$ first part of the formula

RETURN   enters the first part of the formula

Now you will name the first part of the formula. To do this,

Leave your cursor on R7C2 and type:

N   starts NAME command

One   name given to cell

RETURN   executes the command

Now you will be able to enter the formula, in column 2, to the right of Wkly Cash Payment, which will calculate the weekly cash payment.

Place your cursor on R8C2 and type:

V   starts VALUE command

One   part one of the formula

/   divides

$(ar/cp)/((((1 + (ar/cp))^(cp * ny * pp/pp)) - 1)/(ar/cp))$ part two of formula

RETURN   enters the formula

You now need to format the cell into which you have just entered the formula so that it will be displayed with two decimal places. To do this,

Leave your cursor on R8C2 and type:

F	starts FORMAT command
C	selects Cells option and displays R8C2
[TAB] [TAB]	moves cursor to Format Code:
F	selects Fixed option
[TAB]	moves cursor to # of decimals
2	number of decimal places
[RETURN]	executes the command

Now that you have entered all your values and formulas, and named them, your worksheet is complete and should look like Figure 1.

Now that your worksheet is complete, it is ready and all you need to do is enter your own set of known values.

___NOTE___

Never enter values into cells containing formulas, or the formulas will be erased.

SAVING YOUR WORKSHEET

Now save your worksheet for future use, so that the next time you wish to figure this computation all you will need to do is enter in your new known values, and you will not need to retype in the labels or enter the formula.

To save your worksheet, place a formatted data diskette in Drive A.

With your cursor on any location, type:

T	starts TRANSFER command
S	selects Save option

Type in name of file.

[RETURN]	executes the command

PRINTING YOUR WORKSHEET

To print your worksheet, type:

P   starts PRINT command

P   selects Print option and prints

NOTE

If you wish to set an Epson printer to compressed font, type:

P   starts PRINT command

O   selects Options option

TAB   moves cursor to Setup:

^O   sets Epson printer to compressed font
                           Note: type **letter** O

RETURN   prepares for another option selection

P   selects Print option, and prints

LOADING YOUR WORKSHEET BACK INTO MULTIPLAN

At a later date, when you need to use the worksheet to do further computations, just load your worksheet back into memory.

To do this, you must first clear memory if there is anything in it. To clear the memory,

Leave your cursor on any location and type:

T   starts TRANSFER command

C   selects Clear option

Y   Yes, to confirm

Now you are ready to load the worksheet into the memory. To do this,

Place the data diskette from which you wish to load into Drive A.

Leave your cursor on any location and type:

T   starts TRANSFER command

L   selects Load option

Type in the name of the file you wish to load.

RETURN   executes the command

_____ **NOTE** _____

Remember, never enter values into cells containing formulas, or the formulas will be erased.

CHAPTER NINE

AMORTIZING BOND PREMIUM OR DISCOUNT

DESCRIPTION

In this exercise the bond interest expense is computed by using the effective interest rate times the bond book value, rather than the nominal rate times the par value. The cash paid out, however, is computed using the nominal interest rate times par value.

The difference between the interest expense and cash payment is either the bond premium or the discount. Therefore:

If it is a bond premium, then it is subtracted from the bond book value.

If it is a discount, then it is added to the bond book value.

When computing the interest expense for the next period, the adjusted book value is used.

EXAMPLE

A company has a bond with a present value of $93204.84. The coupon/year is 2, the number of periods is 20, the nominal interest rate is 7%, the issue is $100,000 and the payment is $3500. The interest yield is 8% and coupon interest is 4%.

They want an amortization schedule set up for 20 periods which will determine the bond interest expense, the bond discount, and the adjusted book value.

SETTING UP YOUR WORKSHEET - ENTERING LABELS

USE THE FOLLOWING STEP-BY-STEP DIRECTIONS FOR ENTERING THE LABELS IN FIGURE 1:

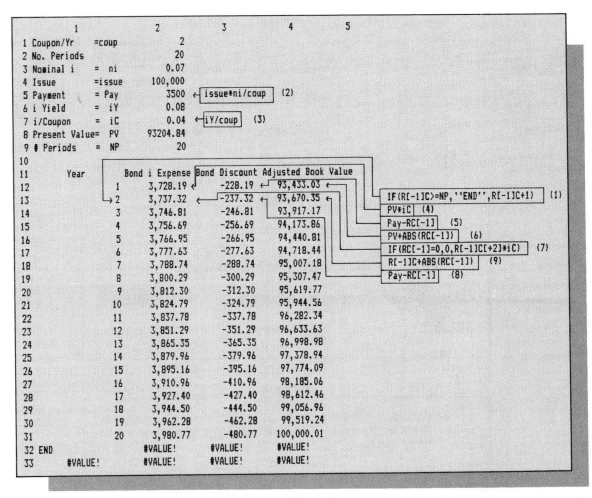

Figure 1

First you need to expand the width of column one to 19 characters. To do this,

Place your cursor on column 1 and type:

F	starts FORMAT command
W	selects Width option
19	column width
RETURN	executes the command

Next you will expand the width of columns two, three and four to 14 characters each. To do this,

Place your cursor on column 2 and type:

F	starts FORMAT command
W	selects Width option
14	column width
TAB TAB	moves cursor to Through:
4	last column to be expanded
RETURN	executes the command

Now type in your labels, after reading the following notes:

_____ **NOTE** _____

Before typing in labels, you must first type:

A   starts ALPHA command which prepares the cell for labeling information

Then type in the label.

RETURN   enters label

_____ **NOTE** _____

DO NOT TYPE in the word "END" in row 32. It will automatically appear there as the result of a formula which you will be entering later in this exercise.

After you have entered all the labels, you will begin entering the known values and naming their locations.

ENTERING AND NAMING VALUES

USE THE FOLLOWING STEP-BY-STEP DIRECTIONS FOR ENTERING AND NAMING THE KNOWN VALUES:

_____ NOTE _____

Naming of cells or groups of cells where values or formulas are placed is only done to make it easier to describe the cells' locations when used in formulas. If you don't name the cells, you can type in the address or point to the cell for cell identification.

Once a cell or a group of cells is named, the name remains, regardless of any labels, values or formulas that may be entered into that location.

In this exercise, we have taken the option of naming some of the cells in order to make the construction of the formula(s) easier to understand.

The first value to enter, in column 2, to the right of coup, is the Coupon/Year.

Place your cursor on R1C2 and type:

| 2 | coupon/year |

| RETURN | enters the value |

Now you will name the cell into which you have just entered the value.

Leave your cursor on R1C2 and type:

| N | starts NAME command |
| coup | name given to cell |

| RETURN | executes the command |

The second value, in column 2, is to the right of No.Period.

Place your cursor on R2C2 and type:

| 20 | number of periods |

| RETURN | enters the value |

It will not be necessary to name the cell into which you have just entered the value. When this value (20) is entered again in row 9, it will be named there.

The third value, in column 2, to the right of ni, is the Nominal interest rate.

Place your cursor on R3C2 and type:

0.07	nominal interest rate

RETURN	enters the value

Now you will name the cell into which you have just entered the value.

Leave your cursor on R3C2 and type:

N	starts NAME command
ni	name given to cell

RETURN	executes the command

The fourth value, in column 2, is to the right of issue.

Place your cursor on R4C2 and type:

100000	issue

RETURN	enters the value

Now you will name the cell into which you have just entered the value.

Leave your cursor on R4C2 and type:

N	starts NAME command
issue	name given to cell

RETURN	executes the command

Now you will format this cell to be displayed with a comma.

Leave your cursor on R4C2 and type:

F	starts FORMAT command
C	selects Cells option

TAB TAB	moves cursor to Format Code:
F	selects Fixed option

RETURN	executes the command
F	starts FORMAT command
O	selects Options option
Y	Yes, for commas

RETURN	executes the command

The fifth value, in column 2, to the right of iY, is the interest yield.

Place your cursor on R6C2 and type:

0.08	interest yield
RETURN	enters the value

Now you will name the cell into which you have just entered the value.

Leave your cursor on R6C2 and type:

N	starts NAME command
iY	name given to cell
RETURN	executes the command

The sixth value, in column 2, to the right of PV, is the present value.

Place your cursor on R8C2 and type:

93204.84	present value
RETURN	enters the value

Now you will name the cell into which you have jsut entered the value.

Leave your cursor on R8C2 and type:

N	starts NAME command
PV	name given to cell
RETURN	executes the command

The seventh value, in column 2, to the right of NP, is the number of periods.

Place your cursor on R9C2 and type:

20	number of periods
RETURN	enters the value

Now you will name the cell into which you have just entered the value.

Leave your cursor on R9C2 and type:

N	starts NAME command
NP	name given to cell
RETURN	executes the command

The eighth and last value to enter, is in column 1, immediately under Year.

Place your cursor on R12C1 and type:

1	first year

RETURN	enters the value

Now that you have entered all the known values, you will enter the formulas.

ENTERING FORMULAS

USE THE FOLLOWING STEP-BY-STEP DIRECTIONS FOR ENTERING THE FORMULAS WHICH WILL CALCULATE THE UNKNOWN VALUES, and name them if the values generated by them are needed in another formula.

Formula one, in column 1, Year, immediately under 1, determines that, if the preceding number is greater than or equal to the number of periods (20), it will display the word "END." If not, it will add 1 to the preceding number.

Place your cursor on R13C1 and type:

V	starts VALUE command
IF (	starts IF function
UP ARROW	moves cursor to 1, and displays R [-1] C
> =	greater than or equal to
NP	number of periods
,	separates expressions
"END"	word to be displayed if above expression is true. Note: Be sure to type the quotation marks before and after the word END.
,	separates expressions
UP ARROW	moves cursor to 1, and displays R [-1] C
+	adds
1	value
)	closes the expressions
RETURN	enters the formula

Formula two, in column 2, to the right of Pay, calculates the payment.

Place your cursor on R5C2 and type:

V	starts VALUE command
issue * ni / coup	formula

RETURN	enters the formula

Now you will name the cell into which you have just entered the formula.

Leave your cursor on R5C2 and type:

N	starts NAME command
Pay	name given to cell

RETURN	executes the command

Formula three, in column 2, to the right of iC, is the interest/coupon.

Place your cursor on R7C2 and type:

V	starts VALUE command
iY/coup	formula

RETURN	enters the formula

Now you will name the cell into which you have just entered the formula.

Leave your cursor on R7C2 and type:

N	starts NAME command
iC	name given to cell

RETURN	executes the command

Formula four, in column 2, immediately under Bond i Expense, multiplies the present value by the interest/coupon.

Place your cursor on R12C2 and type:

V	starts VALUE command
PV * i C	formula

RETURN	enters the formula

You now need to format the cell so that it will be displayed with two decimal places. To do this,

Leave your cursor on R12C2 and type:

F	starts FORMAT command

C	selects Cells option and displays R12C2
TAB TAB	moves cursor to Format Code:
F	selects Fixed option
TAB	moves cursor to # of decimals:
2	number of decimal places
RETURN	executes the command

Formula five in column 3, immediatley under Bond Discount, subtracts the Bond i Expense from the Payment.

Place your cursor on R12C3 and type:

V	starts VALUE command
Pay	payment
—	subtracts
LEFT ARROW	moves cursor to Bond i Expense, and displays RC [-1]
RETURN	enters the formula

You now need to format the cell so that it will be displayed with two decimal places. To do this,

Leave your cursor on R12C3 and type:

F	starts FORMAT command
C	selects Cells option and displays R12C3
TAB TAB	moves cursor to Format Code:
F	selects Fixed option
TAB	moves cursor to # of decimals:
2	number of decimal places
RETURN	executes the command

Formula six in column 4, is immediately under Adjusted Book Value.

Place your cursor on R12C4, and type:

V	starts VALUE command
PV	present value
+	adds

ABS (	converts negative to a positive value, and opens expression.
LEFT ARROW	moves the cursor to Bond Discount and displays RC [-1]
)	closes the expression
RETURN	enters the formula

You now need to format the cell so that it will be displayed with two decimal places. To do this,

Leave your cursor on R12C4 and type:

| F | starts FORMAT command |
| C | selects Cells option and displays R12C4 |

| TAB TAB | moves cursor to Format Code: |
| F | selects Fixed option |

| TAB | moves cursor to # of decimals: |
| 2 | number of decimal places |

| RETURN | executes the command |

Formula seven is in column 2, immediately to the right of Year 2.

Place your cursor on R13C2 and type:

V	starts VALUE command
IF	starts IF function
(	opens expression

LEFT ARROW	moves cursor to 2 (second year), and displays RC [-1]
=0,	equals 0
0,	value selected if true

UP ARROW	
RIGHT ARROW RIGHT ARROW	moves cursor to Adjusted Book Value and displays R [-1] C [+ 2]
*	multiplies
iC	interest/Coupon

|) | closes expression |
| [RETURN] | enters the formula |

You now need to format the cell so that it will be displayed with two decimal places. To do this,

Leave your cursor on R13C2 and type:

| F | starts FORMAT command |
| C | selects Cells option and displays R13C2 |

| [TAB] [TAB] | moves cursor to Format Code: |
| F | selects Fixed option |

| [TAB] | moves cursor to # of decimals: |
| 2 | number of decimal places |

| [RETURN] | executes the command |

Formula eight, in column 3, row 13, which you are about to enter, is the same formula which you entered earlier in R12C3. It is necessary, however, to enter the same formula again in column 3, row 13. To do this,

Place your cursor on R13C3 and type:

V	starts VALUE command
Pay	payment
—	subtracts

| [LEFT ARROW] | moves cursor to Bond i Expense and displays RC [-1] |

| [RETURN] | enters the formula |

You now need to format the cell so that it will be displayed with two decimal places. To do this,

Leave your cursor on R13C3 and type:

| F | starts FORMAT command |
| C | selects Cells option and displays R13C3 |

| [TAB] [TAB] | moves cursor to Format Code: |
| F | selects Fixed option |

| [TAB] | moves cursor to # of decimals |

2	number of decimal places
RETURN	executes the command

Formula nine, is in column 4, Adjusted Book Value column, in row 13.

Place your cursor on R13C4 and type:

V	starts VALUE command
UP ARROW	moves cursor to Adjusted Book Value in row 12 and displays R [-1] C
+	adds
ABS	converts negative value to a positive value
(	opens expression
LEFT ARROW	moves cursor to Bond Discount and displays RC [-1]
)	closes the expression
RETURN	enters the formula

You now need to format the cell so that it will be displayed with two decimal places. To do this,

Leave your cursor on R13C4 and type:

F	starts FORMAT command
C	selects Cells option and displays R13C4
TAB TAB	moves cursor to Format Code:
F	selects Fixed option
TAB	moves cursor to # of decimals
2	number of decimal places
RETURN	executes the command

Now that all your formulas have been entered you will copy **ONLY THE FORMULAS ENTERED INTO ROW 13**, down their respective columns. To do this,

Place your cursor on R13C1 and type:

C	starts COPY command
F	selects From option, and displays R13C1, first cell to copy from

:	colon - indicates from-to
R13C4	last cell to copy from
TAB	moves cursor to To Cells: and displays R13C1, first cell to copy to
:	colon - indicates from-to
R33C1	last cell to copy to
RETURN	executes the command

_____ **NOTE** _____

The word "END" is displayed on row 32, as a result of the formula entered in column 1, row 13.

The word "#VALUE" which you see displayed at the bottom of your worksheet indicates that the formulas have been copied into these cells, allowing you to later add more values as desired. Should any more rows be needed, you will have to copy the formulas down as many columns and rows as needed.

Now that you have entered all your values and formulas, and named them, your worksheet is complete and should look like Figure 1.

Now that your worksheet is complete, it is ready and all you need to do is enter your own set of known values.

_____ **NOTE** _____

Never enter values into cells containing formulas, or the formulas will be erased.

SAVING YOUR WORKSHEET

Now save your worksheet for future use, so that the next time you wish to figure this computation all you will need to do is enter in your new known values, and you will not need to retype in the labels or enter the formula.

To save your worksheet, place a formatted data diskette in Drive A.

With your cursor on any location, type:

T	starts TRANSFER command
S	selects Save option

Type in name of file.

RETURN   executes the command

PRINTING YOUR WORKSHEET

To print your worksheet, type:

P   starts PRINT command

P   selects Print option and prints

_____ **NOTE** _____

If you wish to set an Epson printer to compressed font, type:

P   starts PRINT command

O   selects Options option

TAB   moves cursor to Setup:

ˆO   sets Epson printer to compressed font
                     Note: type **letter** O

RETURN   prepares for another option selection

P   selects Print option, and prints

LOADING YOUR WORKSHEET BACK INTO MULTIPLAN

At a later date, when you need to use the worksheet to do further computations, just load your worksheet back into memory.

To do this, you must first clear memory if there is anything in it. To clear the memory,

Leave your cursor on any location and type:

T   starts TRANSFER command

C   selects Clear option

Y   Yes, to confirm

Now you are ready to load the worksheet into the memory. To do this,

Place the data diskette from which you wish to load into Drive A.

Leave your cursor on any location and type:

T   starts TRANSFER command

L   selects Load option

Type in the name of the file you wish to load.

| RETURN | executes the command

_____ **NOTE** _____

> Remember, never enter values into cells containing formulas, or
> the formulas will be erased.

CHAPTER TEN

EQUIVALENT YIELDS ON TAX-FREE AND TAXABLE BONDS

DESCRIPTION

In some areas municipal and state governments issue bonds which are tax-free. This means you do not have to pay federal income tax on the dividends which you receive. They do not pay a very high rate of interest, but many people feel that the income tax which they save results in a higher yield for them than some of the taxable investments. This exercise determines the equivalent tax yield on a tax free bond (Figure 1), and also the equivalent tax free yield on a taxable bond (Figure 2).

A Tax Free Bond (Figure 1)

EXAMPLE

An individual is considering buying a 6% tax-free yield municipal bond. She is in a 45% income tax bracket.

What taxable yield will she have to earn in order to receive the same amount after taxes?

SETTING UP YOUR WORKSHEET - ENTERING LABELS (For Figure 1)

USE THE FOLLOWING STEP-BY-STEP DIRECTIONS FOR ENTERING THE LABELS IN FIGURE 1:

Column 1 needs to be expanded to allow for the long labels. To do this,

Place your cursor on R1C1 and type:

F   starts FORMAT command

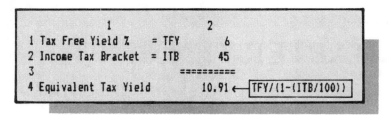

Figure 1

W	selects Width option
25	width of column
RETURN	executes the command

___NOTE___

Before typing in labels, you must first type:

A   starts ALPHA command which prepares the cell for labeling information

Then type in the label.

RETURN   enters label

To enter the double-dashed line in row 3,

Place your cursor on R3C2 and type:

A   starts ALPHA command

= = = = = = = = = =   10 equal signs (=)

RETURN   executes the command

After you have entered all the labels and the double-dashed line, you will begin entering the known values and naming their locations.

ENTERING AND NAMING VALUES

USE THE FOLLOWING STEP-BY-STEP DIRECTIONS FOR ENTERING AND NAMING THE KNOWN VALUES:

NOTE

Naming of cells or groups of cells where values or formulas are placed is only done to make it easier to describe the cells' locations when used in formulas. If you don't name the cells, you can type in the address or point to the cell for cell identification.

Once a cell or a group of cells is named, the name remains, regardless of any labels, values or formulas that may be entered into that location.

In this exercise, we have taken the option of naming some of our cells in order to make the construction of the formula(s) easier to understand.

The first value to enter, in column 2, to the right of TFY, is the Tax Free Yield Percent.

Place your cursor on R1C2 and type:

6	tax free yield %

RETURN	enters the value

Now name the cell into which you have just entered the value.

Leave your cursor on R1C2 and type:

N	starts NAME command
TFY	name given to cell

RETURN	executes the command

The second value, in column 2, to the right of ITB, is the Income Tax Bracket.

Place your cursor on R2C2 and type:

45	income tax bracket

RETURN	enters the value

Now you will name the cell into which you have just entered the value.

Leave your cursor on R2C2 and type:

N	starts NAME command
ITB	name given to cell

RETURN	executes the command

Now that you have entered all the known values, you will enter the formula.

ENTERING THE FORMULA

USE THE FOLLOWING STEP-BY-STEP DIRECTIONS FOR ENTERING THE FORMULA WHICH WILL CALCULATE THE UNKNOWN VALUE:

The formula, in column 2, to the right of Equivalent Tax Yield, calculates the equivalent tax yield you would have to earn to receive the same amount after taxes.

Place your cursor on R4C2 and type:

V	starts VALUE command
TFY / (1 - (ITB / 100))	formula
RETURN	enters the formula

You now need to format the cell so that it will be displayed with two decimal places. To do this,

Leave your cursor on R4C2 and type:

F	starts FORMAT command
C	selects Cells option and displays R4C2
TAB TAB	moves cursor to Format Code:
F	selects Fixed option
TAB	moves cursor to # of decimals:
2	number of decimal places
RETURN	executes the command

Now that you have entered all your values and formulas, and named them, your worksheet is complete and should look like Figure 1.

Now that your worksheet is complete, it is ready and all you need to do is enter your own set of known values.

NOTE

Never enter values into cells containing formulas, or the formulas will be erased.

SAVING YOUR WORKSHEET

Now save your worksheet for future use, so that the next time you wish to figure this computation all you will need to do is enter in your new known values, and you will not need to retype in the labels or enter the formula.

To save your worksheet, place a formatted data diskette in Drive A.

With your cursor on any location, type:

T	starts TRANSFER command
S	selects Save option

Type in name of file.

RETURN	executes the command

PRINTING YOUR WORKSHEET

To print your worksheet, type:

P	starts PRINT command
P	selects Print option and prints

NOTE

If you wish to set an Epson printer to compressed font, type:

P	starts PRINT command
O	selects Options option
TAB	moves cursor to Setup:
O	sets Epson printer to compressed font Note: type **letter** O
RETURN	prepares for another option selection
P	selects Print option, and prints

Now you will clear the memory, in order to proceed with Figure 2 (A Taxable Bond). To do this:

Leave your cursor on any location and type:

T	starts TRANSFER command
C	selects Clear option
Y	yes, to confirm

A Taxable Bond (Figure 2)

EXAMPLE:

In the next exercise, assume that you currently own a taxable bond that pays 10% dividends. You are in a 38% income tax bracket.

What dividend rate will you need to earn in a tax-free bond to get the same return?

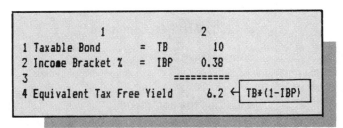

	1	2
1 Taxable Bond	= TB	10
2 Income Bracket %	= IBP	0.38
3		==========
4 Equivalent Tax Free Yield		6.2 ← TB*(1-IBP)

Figure 2

SETTING UP YOUR WORKSHEET - ENTERING LABELS (For Figure 2)

USE THE FOLLOWING STEP-BY-STEP DIRECTIONS FOR ENTERING THE LABELS IN FIGURE 2:

You will need to expand column 1 to accommodate the labels.

Place your cursor on column 1 and type:

F	starts FORMAT command
W	selects Width option
25	width of column
RETURN	executes the command

First type in your labels.

Next enter the double-dashed line in row 3. To do this,

Place your cursor on R3C2 and type:

A	starts ALPHA command
= = = = = = = = = =	10 equal signs (=)
RETURN	executes the command

After you have entered all the labels and the double-dashed line, you will begin entering the known values and naming their locations.

ENTERING AND NAMING VALUES

USE THE FOLLOWING STEP-BY-STEP DIRECTIONS FOR ENTERING AND NAMING THE KNOWN VALUES:

NOTE

Naming of cells or groups of cells where values or formulas are placed is only done to make it easier to describe the cells' locations when used in formulas. If you don't name the cells, you can type in the address or point to the cell for cell identification.

Once a cell or a group of cells is named, the name remains, regardless of any labels, values or formulas that may be entered into that location.

In this exercise, we have taken the option of naming some of the cells in order to make the construction of the formula(s) easier to understand.

The first value to enter, in column 2, to the right of TB, is the dividend rate currently paid on your taxable bond.

Place your cursor on R1C2 and type:

10	dividend rate currently paid

RETURN	enters the value

Now you will name the cell into which you have just entered the value.

Leave your cursor on R1C2 and type:

N	starts NAME command
TB	name given to cell

RETURN	executes the command

The second value, in column 2, to the right of IBP, is the Income Bracket %.

Place your cursor on R2C2 and type:

0.38	income bracket %

RETURN	enters the value

You will now name the cell into which you have just entered the value.

Leave your cursor on R2C2 and type:

N	starts NAME command

I B P	name given to cell
RETURN	executes the command

ENTERING THE FORMULA

USE THE FOLLOWING STEP-BY-STEP DIRECTIONS FOR ENTERING THE FORMULA WHICH WILL CALCULATE THE UNKNOWN VALUE:

The formula in column 2, to the right of Equivalent Tax Free Yield, calculates the dividend rate you need to earn in a tax-free bond to get the same return.

Place your cursor on R4C2 and type:

V	starts VALUE command
T B * (1 — I B P)	formula
RETURN	enters the formula

Now that you have entered all your values and the formula, and named them, your worksheet should look like Figure 2.

Now that your worksheet is complete, it is ready and all you need to do is enter your own set of known values.

____NOTE____

> Never enter values into cells containing formulas, or the formulas will be erased.

SAVING YOUR WORKSHEET

Now save your worksheet for future use, so that the next time you wish to figure this computation all you will need to do is enter in your new known values, and you will not need to retype in the labels or enter the formula.

To save your worksheet, place a formatted data diskette in Drive A.

With your cursor on any location, type:

T	starts TRANSFER command
S	selects Save option

Type in name of file.

RETURN	executes the command

PRINTING YOUR WORKSHEET

To print your worksheet, type:

P   starts PRINT command

P   selects Print option and prints

___NOTE___

If you wish to set an Epson printer to compressed font, type:

P   starts PRINT command

O   selects Options option

TAB   moves cursor to Setup:

^O   sets Epson printer to compressed font

RETURN   prepares for another option selection

P   selects Print option, and prints

LOADING YOUR WORKSHEET BACK INTO MULTIPLAN

At a later date, when you need to use the worksheet to do further computations, just load your worksheet back into memory.

To do this, you must first clear memory if there is anything in it. To clear the memory,

Leave your cursor on any location and type:

T   starts TRANSFER command

C   selects Clear option

Y   Yes, to confirm

Now you are ready to load the worksheet into the memory. To do this,

Place the data diskette from which you wish to load into Drive A.

Leave your cursor on any location and type:

T   starts TRANSFER command

L   selects Load option

Type in the name of the file you wish to load.

RETURN   executes the command

_____ **NOTE** _____

Remember, never enter values into cells containing formulas, or the formulas will be erased.

CHAPTER ELEVEN

COMPUTATION OF REBATE DUE
(Rule of 78's)

DESCRIPTION

When a borrower considers paying off a loan before the end of its original life, he wants to know how much of an interest rebate he will receive, and how much money he will need in order to pay off the loan. The "Rule of 78's" is a formula commonly used in calculating rebate due. Once the rebate due is determined, it is easy to find the payoff amount.

Finding the payoff amount is solved in this exercise in three stages: First the total interest due on the original loan is calculated. Second, using the Rule of 78's, the rebate received for early payoff is computed. Finally, the payoff amount is determined by multiplying the number of payments left by the payment amount, and then subtracting the rebate. The answer is the amount of the payoff.

EXAMPLE

After making 18 payments on his three-year (36 month) car loan, a borrower is contemplating paying off his three-year (36 month) car loan. He originally borrowed $5000 at 5% add-on annual interest, and his monthly payments are $159.72.

If he pays off his loan, how much interest will be rebated, and what amount will pay off his loan?

SETTING UP YOUR WORKSHEET - ENTERING LABELS

USE THE FOLLOWING STEP-BY-STEP DIRECTIONS FOR ENTERING THE LABELS IN FIGURE 1:

For typing in labels which are longer than the width of the cell, utilize Multiplan's Format/Continuous option, which allows you to connect adjacent cells. To do this,

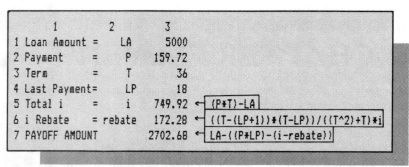

Figure 1

Place your cursor on R1C1 and type:

F	starts FORMAT command
C	selects Cells option and displays R1C1
:	colon - indicates from-to
R7C2	last cell to format
TAB TAB	moves cursor to Format code:
C	selects Continuous option
RETURN	executes the command

─────────── **NOTE** ───────────

Before typing in labels, you must first type:

A   starts ALPHA command which prepares the
         cell for labeling information

Then type in the label.

RETURN   enters label

After you have entered all the labels, you will begin entering the known values and naming their locations.

ENTERING AND NAMING VALUES

USE THE FOLLOWING STEP-BY-STEP DIRECTIONS FOR ENTERING AND NAMING THE KNOWN VALUES:

NOTE

Naming of cells or groups of cells where values or formulas are placed is only done to make it easier to describe the cells' locations when used in formulas. If you don't name the cells, you can type in the address or point to the cell for cell identification.

Once a cell or a group of cells is named, the name remains, regardless of any labels, values or formulas that may be entered into that location.

In this exercise, we have taken the option of naming some of our cells in order to make the construction of the formula(s) easier to understand.

The first value to enter, in column 3, to the right of LA, is the Loan Amount.

Place your cursor on R1C3 and type:

5000	amount of the loan
RETURN	enters the value

Now name the cell into which you have just entered the value.

Leave your cursor on R1C3 and type:

N	starts NAME command
LA	name given to cell
RETURN	executes the command

The second value, in column 3, to the right of P, is the Payment.

Place your cursor on R2C3 and type:

159.72	payment
RETURN	enters the value

Now name the cell into which you have just entered the value.

Leave your cursor on R2C3 and type:

N	starts NAME command

P	name given to cell
RETURN	executes the command

The third value, in column 3, to the right of T, is the Term.

Place your cursor on R3C3 and type:

36	term (months)
RETURN	executes the command

Now name the cell into which you have just entered the value.

Leave your cursor on R3C3 and type:

N	starts NAME command
T	name given to cell
RETURN	executes the command

The fourth value, in column 3, to the right of LP, is the Last Payment.

Place your cursor on R4C3 and type:

18	last payment
RETURN	enters the value

Now name the cell into which you have just entered the value.

Leave your cursor on R4C3 and type:

N	starts NAME command
LP	name given to cell
RETURN	executes the command

Now that you have entered all the known values, you will enter the formulas.

ENTERING THE FORMULAS

USE THE FOLLOWING STEP-BY-STEP DIRECTIONS FOR ENTERING THE FORMULAS
WHICH WILL CALCULATE THE UNKNOWN VALUE, and name them if the values generated
by them are needed in another formula.

Formula one, in column 3, to the right of i, will calculate the total interest due on the original loan.

Place your cursor on R5C3 and type:

(P*T)-LA	formula
RETURN	enters the formula

You will name the cell into which you have just entered the formula.

Leave your cursor on R5C3 and type:

N	starts NAME command
i	name given to cell
RETURN	executes the command

Formula two, in column 3, to the right of rebate, calculates the rebate received for early payoff.
Place your cursor on R6C3 and type:

((T-(LP + 1)) * (T-LP)) / ((T ˆ 2) + T) * i	
RETURN	enters the formula

You will now name the cell into which you have just entered the formula.

Leave your cursor on R6C3 and type:

N	starts NAME command
rebate	name given to cell
RETURN	executes the command

You now need to format the cell so that it will be displayed with two decimal places. To do this,

Leave your cursor on R6C3 and type:

F	starts FORMAT command
C	selects Cells option and displays R8C3
TAB TAB	moves cursor to Format Code:
F	selects Fixed option
TAB	moves cursor to # of decimals:
2	number of decimal places
RETURN	executes the command

Formula three, in column 3, to the right of Payoff Amount, determines the Payoff Amount. Place your cursor on R7C3 and type:

V	starts VALUE command
L A — ((P * L P) — (i — rebate))	formula
RETURN	enters the formula

You now need to format the cell so that it will be displayed with two decimal places. To do this,

Leave your cursor on R7C3 and type:

F	starts FORMAT command
C	selects Cells option and displays R7C3
TAB TAB	moves cursor to Format Code:
F	selects Fixed option
TAB	moves cursor to # of decimals:
2	number of decimal places
RETURN	executes the command

Now that you have entered all your values and formulas, and named them, your worksheet is complete and should look like Figure 1.

Now that your worksheet is complete, it is ready and all you need to do is enter your own set of known values.

_____ **NOTE** _____

Never enter values into cells containing formulas, or the formulas will be erased.

SAVING YOUR WORKSHEET

Now save your worksheet for future use, so that the next time you wish to figure this computation all you will need to do is enter in your new known values, and you will not need to retype in the labels or enter the formula.

To save your worksheet, place a formatted data diskette in Drive A.

With your cursor on any location, type:

T	starts TRANSFER command
S	selects Save option

Type in name of file.

RETURN   executes the command

PRINTING YOUR WORKSHEET

To print your worksheet, type:

P   starts PRINT command

P   selects Print option and prints

_____NOTE_____

If you wish to set an Epson printer to compressed font, type:

P	starts PRINT command
O	selects Options option
TAB	moves cursor to Setup:
^O	sets Epson printer to compressed font Note: type **letter** O
RETURN	prepares for another option selection
P	selects Print option, and prints

LOADING YOUR WORKSHEET BACK INTO MULTIPLAN

At a later date, when you need to use the worksheet to do further computations, just load your worksheet back into memory.

To do this, you must first clear memory if there is anything in it. To clear the memory,

Leave your cursor on any location and type:

T   starts TRANSFER command

C   selects Clear option

Y   Yes, to confirm

Now you are ready to load the worksheet into the memory. To do this,

Place the data diskette from which you wish to load into Drive A.

Leave your cursor on any location and type:

T   starts TRANSFER command

L   selects Load option

Type in the name of the file you wish to load.

| RETURN | executes the command

_____ **NOTE** _____

Remember, never enter values into cells containing formulas, or the formulas will be erased.

CHAPTER TWELVE

CAPITAL ASSET PRICING MODEL

DESCRIPTION

This pricing model is used to derive the expected future return on a security.

EXAMPLE

An analyst is examining a particular security. He knows the risk-free rate of interest, the expected return on the market portfolio of securities, and the volatility of stock return, i.e., the degree of responsiveness relative to that of the market portfolio.

He wants to determine the expected future return on the security for the coming period.

SETTING UP YOUR WORKSHEET - ENTERING LABELS

USE THE FOLLOWING STEP-BY-STEP DIRECTIONS FOR ENTERING THE LABELS IN FIGURE 1:

For typing in labels which are longer than the width of the cell, utilize Multiplan's Format/Continuous option, which allows you to connect adjacent cells. To do this,

Place your cursor on R1C1 and type:

F	starts FORMAT command
C	selects Cells option and displays R1C1
:	colon - indicates from-to
R10C6	last cell to format
TAB TAB	moves cursor to Format code:

```
            1        2        3        4        5        6
 1 Risk-Free Rate Of Interest            =    Rf         6
 2
 3 Expected Return On The Market
 4    Portfolio Of Securities            =    E(Rm)      9
 5
 6 Volatility Of Stock Return            =    B         1.5
 7    (degree of responsiveness relative
 8     to that of the market portfolio)
 9
10 EXPECTED FUTURE RETURN ON THE SECURITY           10.5 ←[ Rf+(ERm-Rf)*B ]
```

Figure 1

| C | selects Continuous option |
| RETURN | executes the command |

NOTE

Before typing in labels, you must first type:

A starts ALPHA command which prepares the cell for labeling information.

Then type in the label.

RETURN enters label

After you have entered all the labels, you will begin entering the known values and naming their locations.

ENTERING AND NAMING VALUES

USE THE FOLLOWING STEP-BY-STEP DIRECTIONS FOR ENTERING AND NAMING THE KNOWN VALUES:

NOTE

Naming of cells or groups of cells where values or formulas are placed is only done to make it easier to describe the cells' locations when used in formulas. If you don't name the cells, you can type in the address or point to the cell for cell identification.

Once a cell or groups of cells is named, the name remains, regardless of any labels, values or formulas that may be entered into that location.

In this exercise, we have taken the option of naming some of our cells in order to make the construction of formula(s) easier to understand.

The first value to enter is the Risk-Free Rate of Interest value, in column 6, to the right of Rf.

To enter the value, place your cursor on R1C6 and type:

6	rate of interest
RETURN	enters the value

Now name the cell into which you have just entered the value.

Leave your cursor on R1C6 and type:

N	starts NAME command
Rf	name of cell
RETURN	executes the command

The second value is the Expected Return On The Market Portfolio Of Securities value, in column 6, to the right of E(Rm).

Place your cursor on R4C6 and type:

9	expected return on market portfolio of securities
RETURN	enters the value

Now name the cell into which you have just entered the value.

Leave your cursor on R4C6 and type:

N	starts NAME command
ERm	name of cell
RETURN	executes the command

The third value is the Volatility Of Stock Return, in column 6, to the right of B.

Place your cursor on R6C6 and type:

1.5	volatility of stock return
RETURN	enters the value

Now name the cell into which you have just entered the value.

Leave your cursor on R6C6 and type:

N	starts NAME command
B	name of cell
RETURN	executes the command

Now that you have entered all the known values, you will enter the formula.

ENTERING THE FORMULA

USE THE FOLLOWING STEP-BY-STEP DIRECTIONS FOR ENTERING THE FORMULA WHICH WILL CALCULATE THE UNKNOWN VALUE.

To enter the formula into column 6, which will calculate the Expected Future Return On The Security,

Place your cursor on R10C6 and type:

V	starts VALUE command
Rf + (ERm-Rf)*B	formula
RETURN	enters the formula

Now that you have entered all your values and the formula, and named them, your worksheet is complete and should look like Figure 1.

Now that your worksheet is complete, it is ready and all you need to do is enter your own set of known values.

___ NOTE ___

Never enter values into cells containing formulas, or the formulas will be erased.

SAVING YOUR WORKSHEET

Now save your worksheet for future use, so that the next time you wish to figure this computation all you will need to do is enter in your new known values, and you will not need to retype in the labels or enter the formula.

To save your worksheet, place a formatted data diskette in Drive A.

With your cursor on any location, type:

T	starts TRANSFER command
S	selects Save option

Type in name of file.

RETURN	executes the command

PRINTING YOUR WORKSHEET

To print your worksheet, type:

P	starts PRINT command
P	selects Print option and prints

_____ **NOTE** _____

If you wish to set an Epson printer to compressed font, type:

P	starts PRINT command
O	selects Options option
TAB	moves cursor to Setup:
O	sets Epson printer to compressed font Note: type **letter** O
RETURN	prepares for another option selection
P	selects Print option, and prints

LOADING YOUR WORKSHEET BACK INTO MULTIPLAN

At a later date, when you need to use the worksheet to do further computations, just load your worksheet back into memory.

To do this, you must first clear memory if there is anything in it. To clear the memory,

Leave your cursor on any location and type:

T	starts TRANSFER command
C	selects Clear option
Y	Yes, to confirm

Now you are ready to load the worksheet into the memory. To do this,

Place the data diskette from which you wish to load into Drive A.

Leave your cursor on any location and type:

| T | starts TRANSFER command |
| L | selects Load option |

Type in the name of the file you wish to load.

| RETURN | executes the command |

_____ **NOTE** _____

Remember, never enter values into cells containing formulas, or the formulas will be erased.

CHAPTER THIRTEEN

ECONOMIC ORDER QUANTITY - INVENTORY MODEL

DESCRIPTION

Economic order quantity means the quantity which needs to be ordered in order to minimize inventory costs during a specified time period, assuming no stockouts. When determining inventory costs, one must consider the ordering costs plus carrying costs. In this exercise, we will determine the economic order quantity and the minimum inventory costs for the time period, as well as the number of times it will be necessary to order.

EXAMPLE

One of the aims of the Woodstock Manufacturing Company is to keep their inventory costs down. They need to order 30,000 units each year. Each purchase order placed costs $18. They have estimated that it costs them $.15 to carry one unit for a year.

The company wants to know what their economic order quantity (EOQ) is, and also what the minimum yearly inventory costs are. They are assuming that their carrying costs will rise to $.25 per unit, and they need to know how the EOQ and their inventory costs will be affected. They also want to know how often it will be necessary to order.

SETTING UP YOUR WORKSHEET - ENTERING LABELS

USE THE FOLLOWING STEP-BY-STEP DIRECTIONS FOR ENTERING THE LABELS IN FIGURE 1:

First expand the width of all your columns. To do this,

Place your cursor on R1C1 and type:

F   starts FORMAT command

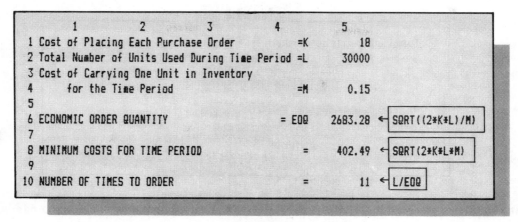

Figure 1

	W			selects Width option

W   selects Width option

12   number of spaces in column

TAB   TAB   moves cursor to Through:

5   number of columns to be expanded

RETURN   executes the command

For typing in labels which are longer than the width of the cell, utilize Multiplan's Format/Continuous option, which allows you to connect adjacent cells. To do this,

Place your cursor on R1C1 and type:

F   starts FORMAT command

C   selects Cells option and displays R1C1

:   colon - indicates from-to

R10C4   last cell to format

TAB   TAB   moves cursor to Format code:

C   selects Continuous option

RETURN   executes the command

_____ **NOTE** _____

Before typing in labels, you must first type:

A   starts ALPHA command which prepares the
                      cell for labeling information

Then type in the label.

[RETURN]   enters label

After you have entered all the labels, you will begin entering the known values and naming their locations.

ENTERING AND NAMING VALUES

USE THE FOLLOWING STEP-BY-STEP DIRECTIONS FOR ENTERING AND NAMING THE KNOWN VALUES:

_____ **NOTE** _____

Naming of cells or groups of cells where values or formulas are placed is only done to make it easier to describe the cells' locations when used in formulas. If you don't name the cells, you can type in the address or point to the cell for cell identification.

Once a cell or a group of cells is named, the name remains, regardless of any labels, values or formulas that may be entered into that location.

In this exercise, we have taken the option of naming some of our cells in order to make the construction of the formula(s) easier to understand.

The first value to enter is in column 5, to the right of K, Cost of Placing Each Purchase Order.

Place your cursor on R1C5 and type:

18   cost of placing each purchase order

[RETURN]   enters the value

Now you will name the cell into which you have just entered the value.

Leave your cursor on R1C5 and type:

N   starts NAME command

K   name given to cell

[RETURN]   executes the command

The second value you will enter is in column 5, to the right of L, Total Number of Units Used During Time Period.

Place your cursor on R2C5 and type:

30000	total number of units used during time period
RETURN	enters the value

You will now name the cell into which you have just entered the value.

Leave your cursor on R2C5 and type:

N	starts NAME command
L	name given to cell
RETURN	executes the command

The third value you will enter is in column 5, to the right of M, Cost of Carrying One Unit in Inventory for the Time Period.

Place your cursor on R4C5 and type:

0.15	cost of carrying one unit in inventory for the time period
RETURN	enters the value

You will name the cell into which you have just entered the value.

Leave your cursor on R4C5 and type:

N	starts NAME command
M	name given to cell
RETURN	executes the command

Now that you have entered all the known values, you will enter the formulas.

ENTERING FORMULAS

USE THE FOLLOWING STEP-BY-STEP DIRECTIONS FOR ENTERING THE FORMULAS WHICH WILL CALCULATE THE UNKNOWN VALUES, and name them if the values generated by them are needed in another formula.

Formula one in column 5, to the right of EOQ, computes the economic order quantity.

Place your cursor on R6C5 and type:

V	starts VALUE command

SQRT((2*K*L)/M)	formula
[RETURN]	enters the formula

You now need to format the cell so that it will be displayed with two decimal points. To do this,

Leave your cursor on R6C5 and type:

F	starts FORMAT command
C	selects Cells option and displays R6C5
[TAB] [TAB]	moves cursor to Format Code:
F	selects Fixed option
[TAB]	moves cursor to # of decimals:
2	number of decimal places
[RETURN]	executes the command

Now you will name the cell into which you have just entered the formula.

Leave your cursor on R6C5 and type:

N	starts NAME command
EOQ	name given to cell
[RETURN]	executes the command

Formula two is in column 5, to the right of Minimum Costs For Time Period.

Place your cursor on R8C5 and type:

V	starts VALUE command
SQRT(2*K*L*M)	formula
[RETURN]	enters the formula

You now need to format the cell so that it will be displayed with two decimal places. To do this,

Leave your cursor on R8C5 and type:

F	starts FORMAT command
C	selects Cells option and displays R8C5
[TAB] [TAB]	moves cursor to Format Code:

F	selects Fixed option
TAB	moves cursor to # of decimals
2	number of decimal places
RETURN	executes the command

Formula three, in column 5, to the right of Times, calculates the number of times to order.

Place your cursor on R10C5 and type:

V	starts VALUE command
L/EOQ	formula
RETURN	enters the formula

Now format the cell into which you have just entered the formula, so that it will read as an integer. To do this,

Leave your cursor on R10C5 and type:

F	starts FORMAT command
C	selects Cells option and displays R10C5
TAB TAB	moves cursor to Format Code:
I	selects Integer option
RETURN	executes the command

Now that you have entered all your values and formulas, and named them, your worksheet is complete and should look like Figure 1.

Now that your worksheet is complete, it is ready and all you need to do is enter your own set of known values.

_____ **NOTE** _____

Never enter values into cells containing formulas, or the formulas will be erased.

SAVING YOUR WORKSHEET

Now save your worksheet for future use, so that the next time you wish to figure this computation all you will need to do is enter in your new known values, and you will not need to retype in the labels or enter the formula.

To save your worksheet, place a formatted data diskette in Drive A.

With your cursor on any location, type:

T   starts TRANSFER command

S   selects Save option

Type in name of file.

| RETURN | executes the command

PRINTING YOUR WORKSHEET

To print your worksheet, type:

P   starts PRINT command

P   selects Print option and prints

NOTE

If you wish to set an Epson printer to compressed font, type:

P   starts PRINT command

O   selects Options option

| TAB | moves cursor to Setup:

^O   sets Epson printer to compressed font
                  Note: type **letter** O

| RETURN | prepares for another option selection

P   selects Print option, and prints

LOADING YOUR WORKSHEET BACK INTO MULTIPLAN

At a later date, when you need to use the worksheet to do further computations, just load your worksheet back into memory.

To do this, you must first clear memory if there is anything in it. To clear the memory,

Leave your cursor on any location and type:

T   starts TRANSFER command

C   selects Clear option

Y   Yes, to confirm

Now you are ready to load the worksheet into the memory. To do this,

Place the data diskette from which you wish to load into Drive A.

Leave your cursor on any location and type:

T   starts TRANSFER command

L   selects Load option

Type in the name of the file you wish to load.

| RETURN | executes the command

_____ **NOTE** _____

> Remember, never enter values into cells containing formulas, or
> the formulas will be erased.

CHAPTER FOURTEEN

COST VOLUME
PROFIT ANALYSIS

DESCRIPTION

In this exercise an analysis of cost-volume-profit includes the determination of the sales volumes (in dollars and cents) needed in order to earn a specified amount after taxes, the after-tax income that would be produced by a specified amount of sales, the breakeven point in sales dollars, and the breakeven point in units sold.

EXAMPLE

The advertising department of a shoe company is planning a sales campaign to promote its new jogging shoes, and wants to determine how much it can budget for the promotion.

Their shoes sell for $20 a pair. The unit variable cost is $15, and the fixed costs in dollars is $3,000. The tax rate percent of income before taxes is 40%. The desired after-tax income is $2500.

They want to determine the unit sales necessary to earn $2500 after taxes, and the after tax income for sales of 1700 units. They also want to know the dollars needed to earn after-tax income ($2500 net), and the after-tax income for sales volume of $34,000. Finally they want to determine the breakeven point in sales dollars, as well as the breakeven point in units.

SETTING UP YOUR WORKSHEET - ENTERING LABELS

USE THE FOLLOWING STEP-BY-STEP DIRECTIONS FOR ENTERING THE LABELS IN FIGURE 1:

First columns 1, 2 and 3 need to be expanded. To do this,

Place your cursor on column 1 and type:

F   starts FORMAT command

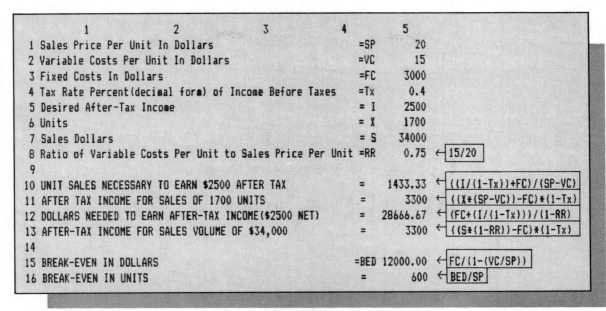

Figure 1

W	selects Width option
16	column width

TAB TAB	moves cursor to Through:
3	columns to be expanded

RETURN	executes the command

Column 4 needs to be expanded to 12 characters. To do this,

Place your cursor on column 4 and type:

F	starts FORMAT command
W	selects Width option
12	column width

RETURN	executes the command

For typing in labels which are longer than the width of the cell, utilize Multiplan's Format/Continuous option, which allows you to connect adjacent cells. To do this,

Place your cursor on R1C1 and type:

F	starts FORMAT command
C	selects Cells option and displays R1C1
:	colon - indicates from-to
R16C4	last cell to format
[TAB] [TAB]	moves cursor to Format code:
C	selects Continuous option
[RETURN]	executes the command

NOTE

Before typing in labels, you must first type:

A   starts ALPHA command which prepares the cell for labeling information

Then type in the label.

[RETURN]   enters label

After you have entered all the labels, you will begin entering the known values and naming their locations.

ENTERING AND NAMING VALUES

USE THE FOLLOWING STEP-BY-STEP DIRECTIONS FOR ENTERING AND NAMING THE KNOWN VALUES:

NOTE

Naming of cells or groups of cells where values or formulas are placed is only done to make it easier to describe the cells' locations when used in formulas. If you don't name the cells, you can type in the address or point to the cell for cell identification.

Once a cell or a group of cells is named, the name remains, regardless of any labels, values or formulas that may be entered into that location.

In this exercise, we have taken the option of naming some of our cells in order to make the construction of the formula(s) easier to understand.

The first value to enter in column 5, to the right of SP, is the Sales Price Per Unit In Dollars.

Place your cursor on R1C5 and type:

20	sales price per unit in dollars

RETURN	enters the value

Now you will name the cell into which you have just entered the value.

Leave your cursor on R1C5 and type:

N	starts NAME command
SP	name given to column

RETURN	executes the command

The second value, in column 5, to the right of VC, is the Variable Costs Per Unit In Dollars.

Place your cursor on R2C5 and type:

15	variable costs per unit in dollars

RETURN	enters the value

Now you will name the cell into which you have just entered the value.

Leave your cursor on R2C5 and type:

N	starts NAME command
VC	name given to cell

RETURN	executes the command

The third value, in column 5, to the right of FC, is the Fixed Costs In Dollars.

Place your cursor on R3C5 and type:

3000	fixed costs in dollars

RETURN	enters the value

Now you will name the cell into which you have just entered the value.

Leave your cursor on R3C5 and type:

N	starts NAME command
FC	name given to cell

RETURN	executes the command

The fourth value, in column 5, to the right of Tx, is the Tax Rate Percent (decimal form) of Income Before Taxes.

Place your cursor on R4C5 and type:

0.4	tax rate of income before taxes

RETURN	enters the value

Now you will name the cell into which you have just entered the value.

Leave your cursor on R4C5 and type:

N	starts NAME command
Tx	name given to cell

RETURN	executes the command

The fifth value, in column 5, to the right of I, is the Desired After-Tax Income.

Place your cursor on R5C5 and type:

2500	desired after-tax income

RETURN	enters the value

Now you will name the cell into which you have just entered the value.

Leave your cursor on R5C5 and type:

N	starts NAME command
I	name given to cell

RETURN	executes the command

The sixth value, in column 5, to the right of X, is the Units sold.

Place your cursor on R6C5 and type:

1700	number of units sold

RETURN	enters the value

Now you will name the cell into which you have just entered the formula.

Leave your cursor on R6C5 and type:

N	starts NAME command
X	name given to cell

RETURN	executes the command

The seventh and last value to enter in column 5, to the right of S, is the Sales Dollars.

Place your cursor on R7C5 and type:

34000	sales dollars

RETURN	enters the value

Now you will name the cell into which you have just entered the value.

Leave your cursor on R7C5 and type:

N	starts NAME command
S	name given to cell

RETURN	executes the command

Now that you have entered all the known values, you will enter the formulas.

ENTERING FORMULAS

USE THE FOLLOWING STEP-BY-STEP DIRECTIONS FOR ENTERING THE FORMULAS WHICH WILL CALCULATE THE UNKNOWN VALUES, and name them if the values generated by them are needed in another formula.

Formula one, in column 5, to the right of RR, is the Ratio of Variable Costs Per Unit to Sales Price Per Unit.

Place your cursor on R8C5 and type:

15/20	variable costs/sales price ratio

RETURN	enters the formula

Now you will name the cell into which you have just entered the formula.

Leave your cursor on R8C5 and type:

N	starts NAME command
RR	name given to cell

RETURN	executes the command

Formula two is in column 5, to the right of Unit Sales Necessary To Earn $2500 After Tax.

Place your cursor on R10C5 and type:

((I / (1-TX)) + FC) / (SP-VC)	formula

RETURN	enters the formula

You now need to format the cell so that it will be displayed with two decimal places. To do this,

Leave your cursor on R10C5 and type:

F	starts FORMAT command
C	selects Cells option and displays R10C5
TAB TAB	moves cursor to Format Code:
F	selects Fixed option
TAB	moves cursor to # of decimals:
2	number of decimal places
RETURN	executes the command

Formula three is in column 5, to the right of After Tax Income For Sales of 1700 Units.

Place your cursor on R11C5 and type:

((X*(SP-VC))-FC)*(1-Tx)	formula
RETURN	enters the formula

Formula four is in column 5, to the right of Dollars Needed To Earn After-Tax Income ($2500 net).

Place your cursor on R12C5 and type:

(F C + (I / (1 — Tx))) / (1 — R R)	formula
RETURN	enters the formula

You now need to format the cell so that it will be displayed with two decimal places. To do this,

Leave your cursor on R12C5 and type:

F	starts FORMAT command
C	selects Cells option and displays R12C5
TAB TAB	moves cursor to Format Code:
F	selects Fixed option
TAB	moves cursor to # of decimals:
2	number of decimal places
RETURN	executes the command

Formula five is in column 5, to the right of After-Tax Income for Sales Volumne of $34,000.

Place your cursor on R13C5 and type:

((S*(1-RR))-FC)*(1-Tx)   formula

RETURN   enters the formula

Formula six, in column 5, to the right of BED, is the Break-Even Amount in Dollars.

Place your cursor on R15C5 and type:

V   starts VALUE command

FC/(1-(VC/SP))   formula

RETURN   enters the formula

Now you will name the cell into which you have just entered the formula.

Leave your cursor on R15C5 and type:

N   starts NAME command

BED   name given to cell

RETURN   executes the command

Formula seven, in column 5, is the break-even amount in units.

Place your cursor on R16C5 and type:

V   starts VALUE command

BED/SP   formula

RETURN   enters the formula

Now that you have entered all your values and formulas, and named them, your worksheet is complete and should look like Figure 1.

Now that your worksheet is complete, it is ready and all you need to do is enter your own set of known values.

_____ **NOTE** _____

Never enter values into cells containing formulas, or the formulas will be erased.

SAVING YOUR WORKSHEET

Now save your worksheet for future use, so that the next time you wish to figure this computation all you will need to do is enter in your new known values, and you will not need to retype in the labels or enter the formula.

To save your worksheet, place a formatted data diskette in Drive A.

With your cursor on any location, type:

T	starts TRANSFER command
S	selects Save option

Type in name of file.

RETURN	executes the command

PRINTING YOUR WORKSHEET

To print your worksheet, type:

P	starts PRINT command
P	selects Print option and prints

_____ **NOTE** _____

If you wish to set an Epson printer to compressed font, type:

P	starts PRINT command
O	selects Options option
TAB	moves cursor to Setup:
ˆO	sets Epson printer to compressed font Note: type **letter** O
RETURN	prepares for another option selection
P	selects Print option, and prints

LOADING YOUR WORKSHEET BACK INTO MULTIPLAN

At a later date, when you need to use the worksheet to do further computations, just load your worksheet back into memory.

To do this, you must first clear memory if there is anything in it. To clear the memory,

Leave your cursor on any location and type:

T	starts TRANSFER command
C	selects Clear option

Y   Yes, to confirm

Now you are ready to load the worksheet into the memory. To do this,

Place the data diskette from which you wish to load into Drive A.

Leave your cursor on any location and type:

T   starts TRANSFER command

L   selects Load option

Type in the name of the file you wish to load.

| RETURN | executes the command

_____ **NOTE** _____

Remember, never enter values into cells containing formulas, or the formulas will be erased.

CHAPTER FIFTEEN

MAINTAINING A STOCK PORTFOLIO

DESCRIPTION

This stock portfolio exercise can be used to compute a purchase gross amount, a market gross amount, the gain in dollars and the gain in percent, as well as the expected return and return ratio.

The high and low estimates and the Beta percentages in this exercise were taken from the Value Line Investment Survey newsletter, which gives you the high and low estimates for a four-year period.

EXAMPLE

The Ashtabula Manufacturing Company has invested some of its profits in 8 securities. They know the purchase prices and market prices of the shares they have purchased, as well as the Beta percentages, and the high and low estimates for their shares.

They want to determine the purchase gross, the market gross, the gain in dollars and the gain in percent, and also the expected return and the return ratio on their investments.

SETTING UP YOUR WORKSHEET - ENTERING LABELS

USE THE FOLLOWING STEP-BY-STEP DIRECTIONS FOR ENTERING THE LABELS IN FIGURE 1:

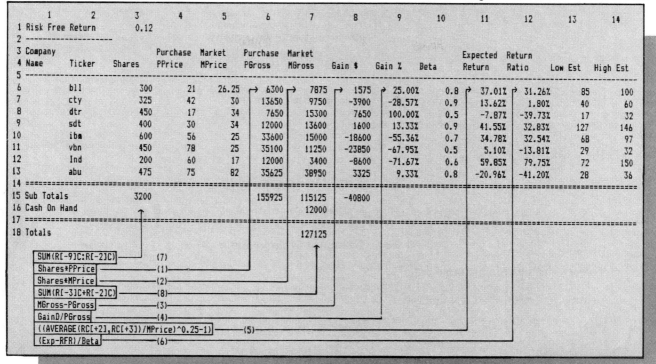

Figure 1

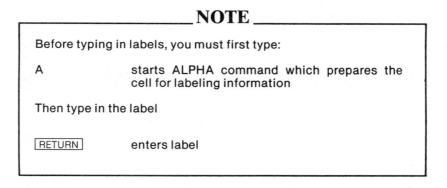

_____ **NOTE** _____

Before typing in labels, you must first type:

A	starts ALPHA command which prepares the cell for labeling information

Then type in the label

RETURN	enters label

First type in the labels, including the labels in column 2, under Ticker.

Next you will want to center the labels in rows 3 and 4. To do this,

Place your cursor on R3C1 and type:

F	starts FORMAT command
C	selects Cells option and displays R3C1
:	colon - indicates from-to
R4C14	last cell to format

TAB	moves cursor to Alignment:
C	selects Center option
RETURN	executes the command

To enter the dashed lines in row 2,

Place your cursor on R2C1 and type:

A	starts ALPHA command
----------	10 dashes
RETURN	executes the command

To copy the dashed line into column 2,

Leave your cursor on R2C1 and type:

C	starts COPY command
R	selects Right option
1	number of cells to copy into
RETURN	executes the command

To enter the dashed line in row 5,

Place your cursor on R5C1 and type:

A	starts ALPHA command
----------	10 dashes
RETURN	executes the command

To copy the dashed line across the row,

Leave your cursor on R5C1 and type:

C	starts COPY command
R	selects Right option
13	number of cells to copy into
RETURN	executes the command

Enter the double-dashed lines in rows 14 and 17 by repeating the above operation, only substituting an equal sign (=) for the dashed sign (-).

After you have entered all the labels, the dashed lines and the double-dashed lines, you will begin entering the known values and naming their locations.

ENTERING AND NAMING VALUES

USE THE FOLLOWING STEP-BY-STEP DIRECTIONS FOR ENTERING AND NAMING THE KNOWN VALUES:

```
_____ NOTE _____

Naming of cells or groups of cells where values or formulas are
placed is only done to make it easier to describe the cells' loca-
tions when used in formulas. If you don't name the cells, you can
type in the address or point to the cell for cell identification.

Once a cell or a group of cells is named, the name remains,
regardless of any labels, values or formulas that may be entered
into that location.

In this exercise, we have taken the option of naming some of the
cells in order to make the construction of the formula(s) easier to
understand.
```

The first value to enter, in column 3, is to the right of Risk Free Return.

Place your cursor on R1C3 and type:

0.12   risk free return

RETURN   enters the value

Now you will name the cell into which you have just entered the value.

Leave your cursor on R1C3 and type:

N   starts NAME command

RFR   name given to cell

RETURN   executes the command

The second group of values, in column 3, between the single and double-dashed lines, is the Shares.

Place your cursor on R6C3 and type:

300   shares

RETURN   enters the value

Continue typing the values down column 3 until you reach the double-dashed line.

Now you will name the column into which you have just entered the values.

Place your cursor on R6C3 and type:

N   starts NAME command

Shares   name given to column

TAB	moves cursor to To Refer To:
R6C3	first cell in column to be named
:	colon - indicates
R13C3	last cell in column to be named
RETURN	executes the command

The third group of values, in column 4, between the single and double-dashed lines, is the Purchase Price.

Place your cursor on R6C4 and type:

21	purchase price
RETURN	enters the value

Continue typing the values down column 4 until you reach the double-dashed line.

Now you will name the column into which you have just entered the values.

Place your cursor on R6C4 and type:

N	starts NAME command
PPrice	name given to column
TAB	moves cursor to To Refer To:
R6C4	first cell in column to be named
:	colon - indicates from-to
R13C4	last cell in column to be named
RETURN	executes the command

The fourth group of values in column 5, between the single and double-dashed lines, is the Market Price.

Place your cursor on R6C5 and type:

26.25	market price
RETURN	enters the value

Now continue typing in the values in column 5, until you reach the double-dashed line.

Now you will name the column into which you have just entered the values.

Place your cursor on R6C5 and type:

N	starts NAME command
MPrice	name given to cell

TAB	moves cursor to To Refer To:
R6C5	first cell in column to be named
:	colon - indicates from-to
R13C5	last cell in column to be named
RETURN	executes the command

The fifth group of values, in column 10, between the single and double-dashed lines, is the Beta.

Place your cursor on R6C10 and type:

0.8	beta
RETURN	enters the value

Continue typing in the values in column 10 until you reach the double-dashed line.

Now you will name the column into which you have just entered the values.

Place your cursor on R6C10 and type:

N	starts NAME command
Beta	name given to cell
TAB	moves cursor to To Refer To:
R6C10	first cell in column to be named
:	colon - indicates from-to
R13C10	last cell in column to be named
RETURN	executes the command

The sixth group of values, in column 13, between the single and double-dashed lines, is the Low Estimate.

Place your cursor on R6C13 and type:

85	low estimate
RETURN	enters the value

Now continue to type in the values in column 13, until you reach the double-dashed line.

You will NOT name this column.

The seventh group of values, in column 14, between the single and double-dashed lines, is the High Estimate.

Place your cursor on R6C14 and type:

100   high estimate

RETURN   enters the value

Continue to type in the values in column 14 until you reach the double-dashed line.

You will NOT name this column.

The eighth and last value to enter, in column 7, is in the Cash On Hand row.

Place your cursor on R16C7 and type:

12000   cash on hand

RETURN   enters the value

Now that you have entered all the known values you will enter the formulas.

ENTERING FORMULAS

USE THE FOLLOWING STEP-BY-STEP DIRECTIONS FOR ENTERING THE FORMULAS WHICH WILL CALCULATE THE UNKNOWN VALUES, and name them if the values generated by them are needed in another formula.

Formula one, in the Purchase Gross column, multiplies the Shares times the Purchase Price.

Place your cursor on R6C6 and type:

V   starts VALUE command

Shares*PPrice   formula

RETURN   enters the formula

Now copy the formula down the column to the double-dashed line. To do this,

Leave your cursor on R6C6 and type:

C   starts COPY command

D   selects Down option

7   number of cells to copy into

RETURN   executes the command

Now you will name the column into which the formulas have just been entered.

Leave your cursor on R6C6 and type:

N   starts NAME command

PGross	name given to column
[TAB]	moves cursor to To Refer To:
R6C6	first cell in column to name
:	colon - indicates from-to
R13C6	last cell in column to name
[RETURN]	executes the command

Formula two, in the Market Gross column, multiplies the Shares times the Market Price.

Place your cursor on R6C7 and type:

V	starts VALUE command
Shares*MPrice	formula
[RETURN]	enters the formula

Now you will copy this formula down the Market Gross column. To do this,

Leave your cursor on R6C7 and type:

C	starts COPY command
D	selects Down option
7	number of cells to copy into
[RETURN]	executes the command

Next you will name the column into which the formulas have just been entered.

Leave your cursor on R6C7 and type:

N	starts NAME command
MGross	name given to column
[TAB]	moves cursor to To Refer To:
R6C7	first cell in column to name
:	colon - indicates from-to
R13C7	last cell in column to name
[RETURN]	executes the command

Formula three, in the Gain $ column, subtracts Purchase Gross from Market Gross.

Place your cursor on R6C8 and type:

V	starts VALUE command
MGross-PGross	formula
RETURN	enters the formula

Now you will copy this formula down the Gain $ column. To do this,

Leave your cursor on R6C8 and type:

C	starts COPY command
D	selects Down option
7	number of cells to copy into
RETURN	executes the command

Now you will name the column into which you have just entered the formulas.

Leave your cursor on R6C8 and type:

N	starts NAME command
GainD	name given to column
TAB	moves cursor to To Refer To:
R6C8	first cell in column to name
:	colon - indicates from-to
R13C8	last cell in column to name
RETURN	executes the command

Formula four, in the Gain % column, gives you the percent of dollars gained, by dividing Gain $ by Purchase Gross.

Place your cursor on R6C9 and type:

V	starts VALUE command
GainD/PGross	formula
RETURN	enters the formula

Next you will format the cell into which you have just entered the formula, so that it will read as a percent with 2 decimal places.

Leave your cursor on R6C9 and type:

F	starts FORMAT command
C	selects Cells option and displays R6C9

TAB TAB	moves cursor to Format Code:
%	selects % option
TAB	moves cursor to # of decimal places
2	number of decimal places
RETURN	executes the command

Next you will copy the formula down the Gain % column.

Leave your cursor on R6C9 and type:

C	starts COPY command
D	selects Down option
7	number of cells to copy into
RETURN	executes the command

It will not be necessary to name this column.

Formula five, in the Expected Return column, first generates the average of the High and Low Estimates, then divides that by the Market Price. Then the result is taken to the .25 power and 1 is subtracted from it, which gives you the percentage per year of a four-year period. The High and Low Estimates, in this exercise, were taken from the Value Line Investment Survey newsletter, which gives you the high and low for a four-year period.

Place your cursor on R6C11 and type:

((AVERAGE(	opens expressions and averages values in the following list
RIGHT ARROW RIGHT ARROW	moves cursor to Low Estimate and displays RC [+2]
,	comma - separates expressions
RIGHT ARROW RIGHT ARROW RIGHT ARROW	moves cursor to High Estimate and displays RC[+3]
)	closes Average function
/	divides
MPrice	Market Price
)	closes expression
^0.25	to the power of 0.25
—1)	subtracts 1 and closes expression
RETURN	enters the formula

Now you will format the cell to read as á percent with 2 decimal places.

Leave your cursor on R6C11 and type:

F	starts FORMAT command
C	selects Cells option and displays R6C11
TAB TAB	moves cursor to Format Code:
%	selects % option
TAB	moves cursor to # of decimals:
2	number of decimal places
RETURN	executes the command

Next you will copy the formula down the Expected Return column.

Leave your cursor on R6C11 and type:

C	starts COPY command
D	selects Down option
7	number of cells to copy into
RETURN	executes the command

Now you will name the column into which you have just entered the formulas.

Leave your cursor on R6C11 and type:

N	starts NAME command
Exp	name given to column
TAB	moves cursor to To Refer To:
R6C11	first cell in column to name
:	colon - indicates from-to
R13C11	last cell in column to name
RETURN	executes the command

Formula six, in the Return Ratio column, subtracts the Risk Free Return from the Expected Return percentage, which is then divided by the Beta percentage. The Beta percentage was taken from the Value Line Investment Survey newsletter.

Place your cursor on R6C12 and type:

(Exp-RFR)/Beta	formula

RETURN	enters the formula

Now you will format the cell to be displayed as a percent with 2 decimal places.

Leave your cursor on R6C12 and type:

F	starts FORMAT command
C	selects Cells option and displays R6C12

TAB TAB	moves cursor to Format Code:
%	selects % option

TAB	moves cursor to # of decimals:
2	number of decimal places

RETURN	executes the command

Next you will copy the formula down the Return Ratio column.

Leave your cursor on R6C12 and type:

C	starts COPY command
D	selects Down option
7	number of cells to copy into

RETURN	executes the command

Formula seven, in the Sub Totals row in the Shares column, adds the total shares.

Place your cursor on R15C3 and type:

V	starts VALUE command
SUM (	adds values in the following list

UP ARROW UP ARROW UP ARROW UP ARROW UP ARROW UP ARROW UP ARROW UP ARROW UP ARROW	moves cursor to first value in the shares column and displays R[-9]C
:	colon - indicates from-to

| UP ARROW |
| UP ARROW | moves cursor to last value in the shares column and displays R[-2]C |

|) | closes expression |

| RETURN | enters the formula |

Now you will want to copy this formula into the Sub Totals row of the Purchase Gross column, the Market Gross column, and the Gain $ column. To do this,

Leave your cursor on R15C3 and type:

| C | starts COPY command |

| F | selects From option, and displays R15C3 |

| TAB | moves cursor to To Cells: |

R15C6,
R15C7,
R15C8

| | cells to copy to |

| RETURN | executes the command |

Formula 8, in the Totals row, Market Gross column, adds the Market Gross subtotal to Cash On Hand.

Place your cursor on R18C7 and type:

| V | starts VALUE command |

| SUM (| adds values in the following list |

| UP ARROW |
| UP ARROW |
| UP ARROW | moves cursor to Market Gross Sub Total and displays R[-3]C |

| + | adds |

| UP ARROW |
| UP ARROW | moves cursor to Cash On Hand and displays R[-2]C |

|) | closes the list |

| RETURN | enters the formula |

Now that you have entered all your values and formulas, and named them, your worksheet is complete and should look like Figure 1.

Now that your workshop is complete, it is ready and all you need to do is enter your own set of known values.

_____ **NOTE** _____

> Never enter values into cells containing formulas, or the formulas
> will be erased.

SAVING YOUR WORKSHEET

Now save your worksheet for future use, so that the next time you wish to figure these computations all you will need to do is enter in your new known values, and you will not need to retype in the labels or enter the formulas.

To save your worksheet, place a formatted data diskette in Drive A.

With your cursor on any location, type:

T	starts TRANSFER command
S	selects Save option

Type in name of file.

RETURN	executes the command

PRINTING YOUR WORKSHEET

To print your worksheet, type:

P	starts PRINT command
P	selects Print option and prints

_____ **NOTE** _____

> If you wish to set an Epson printer to compressed font, type:
>
> | | |
> |---|---|
> | P | starts PRINT command |
> | O | selects Options option |
> | TAB | moves cursor to Setup: |
> | O | sets Epson printer to compressed font
Note: type **letter** O |
> | RETURN | prepares for another option selection |
> | P | selects Print option, and prints |

LOADING YOUR WORKSHEET BACK INTO MULTIPLAN

At a later date, when you need to use the worksheet to do further computations, just load your worksheet back into memory.

To do this, you must first clear memory if there is anything in it. To clear the memory,

Leave your cursor on any location and type:

T	starts TRANSFER command
C	selects Clear option
Y	Yes, to confirm

Now, you are ready to load the worksheet into the memory. To do this,

Place the data diskette from which you wish to load into Drive A.

Leave your cursor on any location and type:

T	starts TRANSFER command
L	selects Load option

Type in the name of the file you wish to load.

RETURN	executes the command

NOTE

Remember, never enter values into cells containing formulas, or the formulas will be erased.

CHAPTER SIXTEEN

COMPUTATIONS FOR TREASURY BILLS

COMPUTATION OF BANK DISCOUNT

DESCRIPTION

Although Treasury bills are widely quoted and traded on a rate basis often called "yield," they are actually quoted and figured on a bank discount basis and many factors must be considered when computing their yield. It is necessary to determine the investment yield on a per annum basis, the investment yield per hundred dollars invested, as well as converting the discount basis to the approximate investment yield.

EXAMPLE

Mr. Andrew Watson is examining a particular Treasury bill which has a dollar price of $91.85 after full discount. The number of days per year used is 360, the discount basis is 8.46% and the days to maturity is 347.

He needs to determine the yield of this bill based on the yield on a per annum basis, the yield per hundred dollars invested, and he will also want to convert the discount basis to the approximate investment yield.

SETTING UP YOUR WORKSHEET - ENTERING LABELS for Figure 1)

USE THE FOLLOWING STEP-BY-STEP DIRECTIONS FOR ENTERING THE LABELS IN FIGURE 1:

Using the following directions, set up your worksheet, as illustrated in Figure 1.

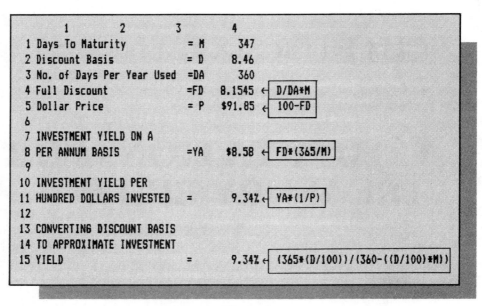

Figure 1

For typing in labels which are longer than the width of the cell, utilize Multiplan's Format/Continuous option, which allows you to connect adjacent cells. To do this,

Place your cursor on R1C1 and type:

F	starts FORMAT command
C	selects Cells option and displays R1C1
:	colon - indicates from-to
R15C3	last cell to format
TAB TAB	moves cursor to Format code:
C	selects Continuous option
RETURN	executes the command

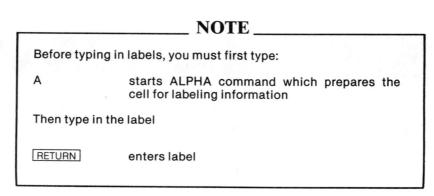

After you have entered all the labels, you will begin entering the known values and naming their locations.

ENTERING AND NAMING VALUES

USE THE FOLLOWING STEP-BY-STEP DIRECTIONS FOR ENTERING AND NAMING THE KNOWN VALUES.

NOTE

Naming of cells or groups of cells where values or formulas are placed is only done to make it easier to describe the cells' locations when used in formulas. If you don't name the cells, you can type in the address or point to the cell for cell identification.

Once a cell or a group of cells is named, the name remains, regardless of any labels, values or formulas that may be entered into that location.

In this exercise, we have taken the option of naming some of our cells in order to make the construction of the formula(s) easier to understand.

The first value to enter in column 4, to the right of M, is the Days To Maturity.

Place your cursor on R1C4 and type:

347	days to maturity

RETURN	enters the value

Now you will name the cell into which you have just entered the value.

Leave your cursor on R1C4 and type:

N	starts NAME command
M	name given to cell

RETURN	executes the command

The second value in column 4, to the right of D, is the Discount Basis.

Place your cursor on R2C4 and type:

8.46	discount basis

RETURN	enters the value

Now you will name the cell into which you have just entered the value.

Leave your cursor on R2C4 and type:

N	starts NAME command

D	name given to cell
RETURN	executes the command

The third value in column 4, to the right of DA, is the No. of Days Per Year Used.

Place your cursor on R3C4 and type:

360	number of days per year used
RETURN	enters the value

Now you will name the cell into which you have just entered the value.

Leave your cursor on R3C4 and type:

N	starts NAME command
DA	name given to cell
RETURN	executes the command

Now that you have entered all the known values, you will enter the formulas.

ENTERING FORMULAS

USE THE FOLLOWING STEP-BY-STEP DIRECTIONS FOR ENTERING THE FORMULAS WHICH WILL CALCULATE THE UNKNOWN VALUES, and name them if the values generated by them are needed in another formula.

Formula one, in column 4, to the right of FD, will determine the full discount per $100 maturity value for a Treasury bill due in 347 days on an 8.46 percent discount basis, based on 360 days per year.

Place your cursor on R4C4 and type:

V	starts VALUE command
D/DA * M	formula
RETURN	enters the formula

You will now name the cell into which you have just entered the formula.

Leave your cursor on R4C4 and type:

N	starts NAME command
FD	name given to cell
RETURN	executes the command

Formula two in column 4, to the right of P, determines the dollar price for that Treasury bill.

Place your cursor on R5C4 and type:

100-FD	formula
RETURN	enters the formula

You now need to format the cell so that it will be displayed in dollars and cents and with two decimal places. To do this,

Leave your cursor on R5C4 and type:

F	starts FORMAT command
C	selects Cells option and displays R5C4
TAB TAB	moves cursor to Format Code:
$	selects $ option
TAB	moves cursor to # of decimals:
2	number of decimal places
RETURN	executes the command

Now you will name the cell into which you have just entered the formula.

Leave your cursor on R5C4 and type:

N	starts NAME command
P	name given to cell
RETURN	executes the command

Formula three, in column 4 to the right of YA, determines the investment yield on a per annum basis. The investment return or yield on a Treasury bill is at a higher rate than the discount basis. In this computation the discount is based on 365 days.

Place your cursor on R8C4 and type:

V	starts VALUE command
FD * (365/M)	formula
RETURN	enters the formula

You now need to format the cell so that it will be displayed in dollars and cents and with two decimal places. To do this,

Leave your cursor on R8C4 and type:

F	starts FORMAT command

C	selects Cells option and displays R8C4
TAB TAB	moves cursor to Format Code:
$	selects $ option
TAB	moves cursor to # of decimals
2	number of decimal places
RETURN	executes the command

Now you will name the cell into which you have just entered the formula.

Leave your cursor on R8C4 and type:

N	starts NAME command
YA	name given to cell
RETURN	executes the command

Formula four, in column 4, to the right of Investment Yield Per Hundred Dollars Invested, determines the investment yield per annum (percentage) per hundred dollars invested.

Place your cursor on R11C4 and type:

V	starts VALUE command
YA * (1/P)	formula
RETURN	enters the formula

You now need to format the cell so that it will be displayed as a percent. To do this,

Leave your cursor on R11C4 and type:

F	starts FORMAT command
C	selects Cells option and displays R11C4
TAB TAB	moves cursor to Format Code:
%	selects % option
TAB	moves cursor to # of decimals:
2	number of decimal places
RETURN	executes the command

Formula five, in column 4, to the right of Converting Discount Basis To Approximate Investment Yield, determines the investment return or yield when converting discount basis to approximate investment yield.

Place your cursor on R15C4 and type:

(365 * (D/100)) / (360 - ((D/100) * M))   formula

RETURN   enters the formula

You now need to format the cell so that it will be displayed as a percent. To do this,

Leave your cursor on R15C4 and type:

F   starts FORMAT command

C   selects Cells option and displays R15C4

TAB TAB   moves cursor to Format Code:

%   selects % option

TAB   moves cursor to # of decimals:

2   number of decimal places

RETURN   executes the command

Now that you have entered all your values and formulas, and named them, your worksheet is complete and should look like Figure 1.

Now that your worksheet is complete, it is ready and all you need to do is enter your own set of known values.

NOTE

Never enter values into cells containing formulas, or the formulas will be erased.

SAVING YOUR WORKSHEET

Now save your worksheet for future use, so that the next time you wish to figure this computation all you will need to do is enter in your new known values, and you will not need to retype in the labels or enter the formulas.

To save your worksheet, place a formatted data diskette in Drive A.

With your cursor on any location, type:

T   starts TRANSFER command

S   selects Save option

Type in name of file.

RETURN   executes the command

PRINTING YOUR WORKSHEET

To print your worksheet, type:

P   starts PRINT command

P   selects Print option and prints

NOTE

If you wish to set an Epson printer to compressed font, type:

P   starts PRINT command

O   selects Options option

TAB   moves cursor to Setup:

^O   sets Epson printer to compressed font
                     Note: type **letter** O

RETURN   prepares for another option selection

P   selects Print option, and prints

To proceed with Figure 2, you will need to clear the memory. To do this,

Leave your cursor on any location and type:

T   starts TRANSFER command

C   selects Clear option

Y   Yes, to confirm

TREASURY BILL RETURNS (Figure 2)

DESCRIPTION

U.S. Treasury bills are frequently sold prior to maturity at a rate basis different from that at which they were purchased. Investors may desire to determine the return from bills under such conditions, or how long bills need to be held to avoid loss. The following formulas can be used for those calculations in most situations. For extreme accuracy, where large amounts are involved, the investor should refer to the computation tables and formulas issued by the Treasury Department in Circular No. 300, Fourth Revision.

EXAMPLE

Mr. Watson now wants to examine another type of treasury bill. He knows the number of days to maturity (347), the original rate of discount (8.46), the number of days held (45), and the difference between the rate at which bills are purchased and that at which they are sold (40%).

He needs to determine the alteration in the original cost resulting from the difference between the purchase price and the sale price over the period held. He also needs to know the return for the period held, and at what rate the bills must be sold.

SETTING UP YOUR WORKSHEET - ENTERING LABELS
for Figure 2)

USE THE FOLLOWING STEP-BY-STEP DIRECTIONS FOR ENTERING THE LABELS IN FIGURE 2:

```
              1         2         3         4        5        6
 1 Number Of Days To Maturity Of Treasury
 2 Bills When Purchased                            =  MA      347
 3
 4 Original Rate Of Discount                       = rate     8.46
 5
 6 Number Of Days Held                             =  da      45
 7
 8 Difference Between The Rate At Which
 9 Bills Are Purchased And That At Which
10 They Are Sold                                   = DIFF     0.4
11
12 ALTERATION IN ORIGINAL COST (RATE)
13 RESULTING FROM DIFFERENCE BETWEEN PURCHASE
14 PRICE AND SALE PRICE OVER PERIOD HELD           =  A       2.68  ← (MA-da)/da*DIFF
15
16 RETURN FOR PERIOD HELD                          =         11.14  ← rate+A
17
18 THEREFORE, BILLS MUST BE SOLD AT                =          8.06  ← rate-DIFF
```

Figure 2

For typing in labels which are longer than the width of the cell, utilize Multiplan's Format/Continuous option, which allows you to connect adjacent cells. To do this,

Place your cursor on R1C1 and type:

F   starts FORMAT command

C   selects Cells option and displays R1C1

:	colon - indicates from-to
R18C5	last cell to format
TAB TAB	moves cursor to Format code:
C	selects Continuous option
RETURN	executes the command

NOTE

Before typing in labels, you must first type:

A   starts ALPHA command which prepares the cell for labeling information

Then type in the label

RETURN   enters label

After you have entered all the labels, you will begin entering the known values and naming their locations.

ENTERING AND NAMING VALUES

USE THE FOLLOWING STEP-BY-STEP DIRECTIONS FOR ENTERING AND NAMING THE KNOWN VALUES.

NOTE

Naming of cells or groups of cells where values or formulas are placed is only done to make it easier to describe the cells' locations when used in formulas. If you don't name the cells, you can type in the address or point to the cell for cell identification.

Once a cell or a group of cells is named, the name remains, regardless of any labels, values or formulas that may be entered into that location.

In this exercise, we have taken the option of naming some of our cells in order to make the construction of the formula(s) easier to understand.

The first value to enter in column 6, to the right of MA, is the Number of Days To Maturity Of Treasury Bills When Purchased.

Place your cursor on R2C6 and type:

347	number of days to maturity of bills when purchased.
RETURN	enters the value

Now you will name the cell into which you have just entered the value.

Leave your cursor on R2C6 and type:

N	starts NAME command
MA	name given to cell
RETURN	executes the command

The second value in column 6, to the right of rate, is the Original Rate Of Discount.

Place your cursor on R4C6 and type:

8.46	original rate of discount
RETURN	enters the value

Now you will name the cell into which you have just entered the value.

Leave your cursor on R4C6 and type:

N	starts NAME command
rate	name given to cell
RETURN	executes the command

The third value in column 6, to the right of da, is the Number of Days Held.

Place your cursor on R6C6 and type:

45	number of days held
RETURN	enters the value

You will now name the cell into which you have just entered the value.

Leave your cursor on R6C6 and type:

N	starts NAME command
da	name given to cell
RETURN	executes the command

The fourth value in column 6, to the right of DIFF, is the Difference Between The Rate At Which Bills Are Purchased and That at Which They Are Sold.

Place your cursor on R10C6 and type:

0.4	difference between rate at which purchased and rate at which sold
RETURN	enters the value

You will now name the cell into which you have just entered the value.

Leave your cursor on R10C6 and type:

N	starts NAME command
DIFF	name given to cell
RETURN	executes the command

Now that you have entered all the known values, you will enter the formulas.

ENTERING FORMULAS

USE THE FOLLOWING STEP-BY-STEP DIRECTIONS FOR ENTERING THE FORMULAS WHICH WILL CALCULATE THE UNKNOWN VALUES, and name them if the values generated by them are needed in another formula.

Formula one, in column 6, to the right of A, shows how original rate of 8.46% was altered by 2.6844%. Since bills were sold at a rate basis lower than the cost, representing a gain, the original rate was increased and the figure of 2.6844% represents an addition.

Place your cursor on R14C6 and type:

(MA-da)/da * DIFF	formula
RETURN	enters the formula

You will now need to format the cell so that it will be displayed with two decimal places. To do this,

Leave your cursor on R14C6 and type:

F	starts FORMAT command
C	selects Cells option and displays R14C6
TAB TAB	moves cursor to Format Code:
F	selects Fixed option
TAB	moves cursor to # of decimals:
2	number of decimal places
RETURN	executes the command

You will now name the cell into which you have just entered the formula.

Leave your cursor on R14C6 and type:

N	starts NAME command
A	name given to cell
RETURN	executes the command

Formula two in column 6, to the right of Return For Period Held, adds original rate (8.46) to alteration (2.6844) and arrives at return for period held.

Place your cursor on R16C6 and type:

V	starts VALUE command
rate + A	formula
RETURN	enters the formula

You now need to format the cell so that it will be displayed with two decimal places. To do this,

Leave your cursor on R16C6 and type:

F	starts FORMAT command
C	selects Cells option and displays R16C6
TAB TAB	moves cursor to Format Code:
F	selects Fixed option
TAB	moves cursor to # of decimals:
2	number of decimal places
RETURN	executes the command

Formula three, in column 6 to the right of Therefore, Bills Must Be Sold At, shows the difference between purchase price and sale price necessary to show a return of 10.4733 percent, and illustrates that the bills must be sold at 8.46% minus .40%, or 8.06%.

Place your cursor on R18C6 and type:

V	starts VALUE command
rate—DIFF	formula
RETURN	enters the formula

Now that you have entered all your values and formulas, and named them, your worksheet is complete and should look like Figure 1.

Now that your worksheet is complete, it is ready and all you need to do is enter your own set of known values.

```
_____ NOTE _____
Never enter values into cells containing formulas, or the formulas
will be erased.
```

SAVING YOUR WORKSHEET

Now save your worksheet for future use, so that the next time you wish to figure this computation all you will need to do is enter in your new known values, and you will not need to retype in the labels or enter the formula.

To save your worksheet, place a formatted data diskette in Drive A.

With your cursor on any location, type:

T	starts TRANSFER command
S	selects Save option

Type in name of file.

RETURN	executes the command

PRINTING YOUR WORKSHEET

To print your worksheet, type:

P	starts PRINT command
P	selects Print option and prints

```
_____ NOTE _____
If you wish to set an Epson printer to compressed font, type:

P          starts PRINT command

O          selects Options option

TAB        moves cursor to Setup:

^O         sets Epson printer to compressed font
           Note: type letter O


RETURN     prepares for another option selection

P          selects Print option, and prints
```

LOADING YOUR WORKSHEET BACK INTO MULTIPLAN

At a later date, when you need to use the worksheet to do further computations, just load your worksheet back into memory.

To do this, you must first clear memory if there is anything in it. To clear the memory,

Leave your cursor on any location and type:

T	starts TRANSFER command
C	selects Clear option
Y	Yes, to confirm

Now you are ready to load the worksheet into the memory. To do this,

Place the data diskette from which you wish to load into Drive A.

Leave your cursor on any location and type:

T	starts TRANSFER command
L	selects Load option

Type in the name of the file you wish to load.

RETURN	executes the command

_____ **NOTE** _____

> Remember, never enter values into cells containing formulas, or the formulas will be erased.

CHAPTER SEVENTEEN

FINDING THE MEAN, STANDARD DEVIATION, AND VARIANCE OF A POPULATION

DESCRIPTION

When a set of data is set up for study, statistical calculations are used to explain and describe the data. One of the most common computations is determining the mean, or average, of the data given. Another useful calculation is finding the standard deviation, (commonly referred to as the spread or distribution of the data points). It is also useful to know the extent to which, or range in which, a thing varies, which is called the variance.

EXAMPLE

A word processing school gives periodic tests to its students in order to assess their advancement. The highest possible score in the test is 10. The test was given to 5 of the students.

The school now needs to know the mean, the standard deviation, and the variance.

SETTING UP YOUR WORKSHEET - ENTERING LABELS

USE THE FOLLOWING STEP-BY-STEP DIRECTIONS FOR ENTERING THE LABELS IN FIGURE 1:

```
_____ NOTE _____

Before typing in labels, you must first type:

A              starts ALPHA command which prepares the
               cell for labeling information

Then type in the label.

RETURN         enters label
```

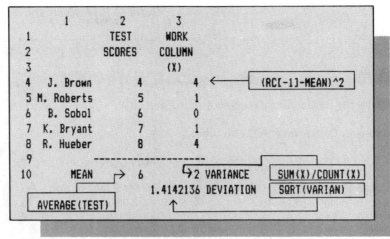

Figure 1

To center the labels at the top of columns 2 and 3,

Place your cursor on R1C2 and type:

F	starts FORMAT command
C	selects Cells option and displays R1C2
:	colon - indicates from-to
R3C3	last cell to format
TAB	moves cursor to Alingment: options
C	selects Center option
RETURN	executes the command

To right-justify the labels in column 1, place your cursor on R4C1 and type:

F	starts FORMAT command
C	selects Cells option and displays R4C1
:	colon - indicates from-to
R10C1	last cell to format
TAB	moves cursor to Alignment: options
R	selects Right option
RETURN	executes the command

Now enter the dashed lines in row 9. To do this,

Place your cursor on R9C2 and type:

A	starts ALPHA command
----------	10 dashes
RETURN	enters the dashes

To copy the dashed line over to column 3 in row 9,

Leave your cursor on R9C2 and type:

C	starts COPY command
R	selects Right option
1	number of cells to copy into
RETURN	executes the command

After you have entered all the labels and the dashed lines, you will begin entering the known values and naming their locations.

ENTERING AND NAMING VALUES

USE THE FOLLOWING STEP-BY-STEP DIRECTIONS FOR ENTERING AND NAMING THE KNOWN VALUES.

NOTE

Naming of cells or groups of cells where values or formulas are placed is only done to make it easier to describe the cells' locations when used in formulas. If you don't name the cells, you can type in the address or point to the cell for cell identification.

Once a cell or a group of cells is named, the name remains, regardless of any labels, values or formulas that may be entered into that location.

In this exercise, we have taken the option of naming some of our cells in order to make the construction of the formula(s) easier to understand.

The first value to enter is in column 2, immediately to the right of J. Brown. To enter this value,

Place your cursor on R4C2 and type:

4	test score for J. Brown
RETURN	enters the value

Continue to enter the test scores in column 2, ABOVE the dashed line.

Next you will name the test scores you have just entered.

Place your cursor on R4C2 and type:

N	starts NAME command
TEST	name given to cells
TAB	moves cursor to R4C2, first cell in column to name
:	colon - indicates from-to
R8C2	last cell in column to name
RETURN	executes the command

Now that you have entered all the known values, you will enter the formulas.

ENTERING FORMULAS

USE THE FOLLOWING STEP-BY-STEP DIRECTIONS FOR ENTERING THE FORMULAS WHICH WILL CALCULATE THE UNKNOWN VALUES, and name them if the values generated by them are needed in another formula.

Formula one, in column 2, to the right of MEAN, immediately underneath the dashed line, will calculate the mean.

Place your cursor on R10C2 and type:

V	starts VALUE command
AVERAGE(TEST)	formula
RETURN	enters the formula

Now you will name the cell into which you have just entered the formula.

Leave your cursor on R10C2 and type:

N	starts NAME command
MEAN	name given to cell
TAB	moves cursor to To Refer To:
R10C2	cell to be named
RETURN	executes the command

Formula two, in column 3, will generate the variance.

Place your cursor on R4C3 and type:

(	opens the expression
LEFT ARROW	moves cursor to first test score, and displays RC[-1]

—	subtracts
MEAN	value to subtract
)	closes the expression
ˆ2	the power of 2
RETURN	enters the formula

Now you will need to copy this formula down Work Column (X) to the dashed line.

To do this,

Leave your cursor on R4C3 and type:

C	starts COPY command
D	selects Down option
4	number of cells to copy into
RETURN	executes the command

Now you will name the column into which you have just entered the formula. To do this,

Leave your cursor on R4C3 and type:

N	starts NAME command
X	name given to column
TAB	moves cursor to R4C3, first cell in column to name
:	colon - indicates from-to
R8C8	last cell in column to name
RETURN	executes the command

Formula three, in column 3, to the left of Variance, immediately underneath the dashed line, calculates the variance.

Place your cursor on R10C3 and type:

V	starts VALUE command
SUM(X)/COUNT(X)	formula
RETURN	enters the formula

Now you will name the cell into which you have just entered the formula.

N	starts NAME command

VARIAN	name given to cell

RETURN	executes the command

Formula four, in column three, to the left of Deviation, calculates the standard deviation.

Place your cursor on R11C3 and type:

V	starts VALUE command

SQRT(VARIAN)	formula

RETURN	enters the formula

Now that you have entered all your values and formulas, and named them, your worksheet is complete and should look like Figure 1.

Now that your worksheet is complete, it is ready and all you need to do is enter your own set of known values.

NOTE

Never enter values into cells containing formulas, or the formulas will be erased.

SAVING YOUR WORKSHEET

Now save your worksheet for future use, so that the next time you wish to figure these computations all you will need to do is enter in your new known values, and you will not need to retype in the labels or enter the formulas.

To save your worksheet, place a formatted data diskette in Drive A.

With your cursor on any location, type:

T	starts TRANSFER command

S	selects Save option

Type in name of file.

RETURN	executes the command

PRINTING YOUR WORKSHEET

To print your worksheet, type:

P	starts PRINT command

P	selects Print option and prints

NOTE

If you wish to set an Epson printer to compressed font, type:

P	starts PRINT command
O	selects Options option
TAB	moves cursor to Setup:
ˆO	sets Epson printer to compressed font Note: type **letter** O
RETURN	prepares for another option selection
P	selects Print option, and prints

LOADING YOUR WORKSHEET BACK INTO MULTIPLAN

At a later date, when you need to use the worksheet to do further computations, just load your worksheet back into memory.

To do this, you must first clear memory if there is anything in it. To clear the memory,

Leave your cursor on any location and type:

T	starts TRANSFER command
C	selects Clear option
Y	Yes, to confirm

Now you are ready to load the worksheet into the memory. To do this,

Place the data diskette from which you wish to load into Drive A.

Leave your cursor on any location and type:

T	starts TRANSFER command
L	selects Load option

Type in the name of the file you wish to load.

RETURN	executes the command

NOTE

Remember, never enter values into cells containing formulas, or the formulas will be erased.

CHAPTER EIGHTEEN

FINDING THE MEAN, STANDARD DEVIATION, AND STANDARD ERROR OF MEAN FOR A SAMPLE

DESCRIPTION

When a set of statistics which has been derived from a sampling is being studied, certain calculations have to be performed in order to fully evaluate the meaning of the statistics. It is advisable to calculate the mean, the standard error of that mean, as well as the standard deviation, of the statistics being analyzed.

EXAMPLE

A retail chain store has two top salespersons. The manager wants to compare the daily sales of its two star salespersons for a 20-day period.

He wants to know what the average daily sales of each salesperson are, and the standard deviation of each salesperson's sales, as well as the standard error of mean.

SETTING UP YOUR WORKSHEET - ENTERING LABELS

USE THE FOLLOWING STEP-BY-STEP DIRECTIONS FOR ENTERING THE LABELS IN FIGURE 1:

First expand all your columns to 12 spaces.

Place your cursor on column 1 and type:

F	starts FORMAT command
W	selects Width option
12	number of spaces in column

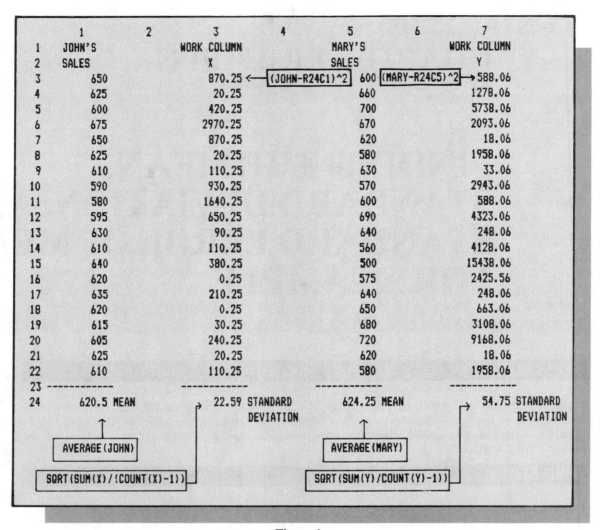

Figure 1

TAB TAB	moves cursor to Through:
7	number of columns to be expanded
RETURN	executes the command

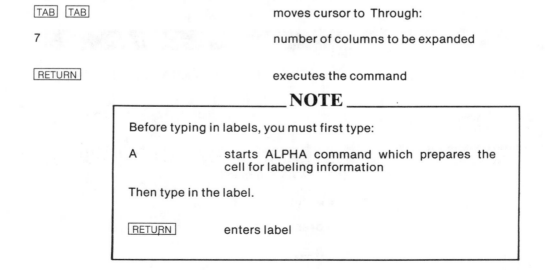

───── **NOTE** ─────

Before typing in labels, you must first type:

A   starts ALPHA command which prepares the cell for labeling information

Then type in the label.

RETURN   enters label

To center the labels in rows 1 and 2,

Place your cursor on R1C1 and type:

F	starts FORMAT command
C	selects Cells option and displays R1C1
:	colon - indicates from-to
R2C7	last cell to format
TAB	moves cursor to Alignment:
C	selects Center option
RETURN	executes the command

To enter the dashed lines,

Place your cursor on R23C1 and type:

A	starts ALPHA command
------------	12 dashes
RETURN	enters the dashed line

Now copy the dashed lines into columns 3, 5 and 7 in row 23.

Leave your cursor on R23C1 and type:

C	starts COPY command
F	selects From option
TAB	moves cursor to To cells:
R23C3, R23C5, R23C7	cells to copy into
RETURN	executes the command

After you have entered all the labels, and the dashed lines, you will begin entering the known values and naming their locations.

ENTERING AND NAMING VALUES

USE THE FOLLOWING STEP-BY-STEP DIRECTIONS FOR ENTERING AND NAMING THE KNOWN VALUES:

_____ **NOTE** _____

Naming of cells or groups of cells where values or formulas are placed is only done to make it easier to describe the cells' locations when used in formulas. If you don't name the cells, you can type in the address or point to the cell for cell identification.

Once a cell or a group of cells is named, the name remains, regardless of any labels, values or formulas that may be entered into that location.

In this exercise, we have taken the option of naming some of our cells in order to make the construction of the formula(s) easier to understand.

The first value to enter is in column 1, immediately underneath John's Sales.

Place your cursor on R3C1 and type:

650	John's sales for first day

RETURN	enters the value

Continue entering John's Sales in column 1, until you reach the dashed line.

Now you will name the column into which you have just entered the values.

Place your cursor on R3C1 and type:

N	starts NAME command
JOHN	name given to column

TAB	moves cursor to To Refer To:
R3C1	first cell in column to name
:	colon - indicates from-to
R22C1	last cell in column to name

RETURN	executes the command

The second group of values to enter is in column 5, immediately underneath Mary's Sales. To do this,

Place your cursor on R3C5 and type:

600	Mary's sales for first day

RETURN	enters the value

Continue to enter Mary's Sales in column 5, down to the dashed line.

Now you will name the column into which you have just entered Mary's Sales.

Place your cursor on R3C5 and type:

N	starts NAME command
MARY	name given to column
TAB	moves cursor to To Refer To:
R3C5	first cell in column to name
:	colon - indicates from-to
R22C5	last cell in column to name
RETURN	executes the command

Now that you have entered all the known values, you will enter the formulas.

ENTERING FORMULAS

USE THE FOLLOWING STEP-BY-STEP DIRECTIONS FOR ENTERING THE FORMULAS WHICH WILL CALCULATE THE UNKNOWN VALUES, and name them if the values generated by them are needed in another formula.

Formula one, in column 1, to the left of MEAN, immediately underneath the dashed line, calculates John's Mean.

Place your cursor on R24C1 and type:

V	starts VALUE command
AVERAGE(JOHN)	formula
RETURN	enters the formula

Formula two, in column 5, to the left of MEAN, immediately underneath the dashed line, calculates Mary's Mean.

Place your cursor on R24C5 and type:

V	starts VALUE command
AVERAGE(MARY)	formula
RETURN	enters the command

Formula three, in column 3, immediately underneath Work Column X, calculates John's standard deviation.

Place your cursor on R3C3 and type:

(JOHN-R24C1)^2	formula
RETURN	enters the formula

Now you will copy this formula down the column to the dashed line.

Leave your cursor on R3C3 and type:

C	starts COPY command
F	selects From option and displays R3C3
TAB	moves cursor to To Cells:
R3C3	first cell to copy to
:	colon - indicates from-to
R22C3	last cell to copy to
RETURN	executes the command

Next you will name the column into which you have just entered the formula.

Leave your cursor on R3C3 and type:

N	starts NAME command
X	name given to column
TAB	moves cursor to To Refer To:
R3C3	first cell in column to name
:	colon - indicates from-to
R22C3	last cell in column to name
RETURN	executes the command

Formula four in column 7, immediately underneath Work Column Y, determines Mary's standard deviation.

Place your cursor on R3C7 and type:

(MARY-R24C5)^2	formula
RETURN	enters the formula

You now need to format the cell so that it will be displayed with two decimal places. To do this,

Leave your cursor on R3C7 and type:

F	starts FORMAT command
C	selects Cells option and displays R3C7

TAB TAB	moves cursor to Format Code:
F	selects Fixed option
TAB	moves cursor to # of decimals:
2	number of decimal places
RETURN	executes the command

Now copy this formula down Work Column Y to the dashed line.

Leave your cursor on R3C7 and type:

C	starts COPY command
F	selects From option and displays R3C7, cell to copy from
TAB	moves cursor to To Cells:
R3C7	first cell to copy to
:	colon - indicates from-to
R22C7	last cell to copy to
RETURN	executes the command

Now you will name Work Column Y into which you have just entered the formulas.

Leave your cursor on R3C7 and type:

N	starts NAME command
Y	name given to column
TAB	moves cursor to To Refer To:
R3C7	First cell in column to name
:	colon - indicates from-to
R22C7	last cell in column to name
RETURN	executes the command

Formula five in column 3, Work Column X, below the dashed line, calculates the standard deviation for John's Sales.

Place your cursor on R24C3 and type:

V	starts VALUE command

SQRT(SUM(X)/(COUNT(X)-1))	formula
RETURN	enters the formula

You now need to format the cell so that it will be displayed with two decimal places. To do this,

Leave your cursor on R24C3 and type:

F	starts FORMAT command
C	selects Cells option and displays R24C3
TAB TAB	moves cursor to Format Code:
F	selects Fixed option
TAB	moves cursor to # of decimals:
2	number of decimal places
RETURN	executes the command

Formula six, in column 7, in Work Column Y, below the dashed line, calculates the standard deviation for Mary's sales.

Place your cursor on R24C7 and type:

V	starts VALUE command
SQRT(SUM(Y)/(COUNT(Y)-1))	formula
RETURN	enters the formula

You now need to format the cell so that it will be displayed with two decimal places. To do this,

Leave your cursor on R24C7 and type:

F	starts FORMAT command
C	selects Cells option and displays R24C7
TAB TAB	moves cursor to Format Code:
F	selects Fixed option
TAB	moves cursor to # of decimals:
2	number of decimal places
RETURN	executes the command

Now that you have entered all your values and formulas, and named them, your worksheet is complete and should look like Figure 1.

Now that your worksheet is complete, it is ready and all you need to do is enter your own set of known values.

NOTE

Never enter values into cells containing formulas, or the formulas will be erased.

SAVING YOUR WORKSHEET

Now save your worksheet for future use, so that the next time you wish to figure this computation all you will need to do is enter in your new known values, and you will not need to retype in the labels or enter the formula.

To save your worksheet, place a formatted data diskette in Drive A.

With your cursor on any location, type:

T	starts TRANSFER command
S	selects Save option

Type in name of file.

RETURN	executes the command

PRINTING YOUR WORKSHEET

To print your worksheet, type:

P	starts PRINT command
P	selects Print option and prints

NOTE

If you wish to set an Epson printer to compressed font, type:

P	starts PRINT command
O	selects Options option
TAB	moves cursor to Setup:
O	sets Epson printer to compressed font Note: type **letter** O
RETURN	prepares for another option selection
P	selects Print option, and prints

LOADING YOUR WORKSHEET BACK INTO MULTIPLAN

At a later date, when you need to use the worksheet to do further computations, just load your worksheet back into memory.

To do this, you must first clear memory if there is anything in it. To clear the memory,

Leave your cursor on any location and type:

T	starts TRANSFER command
C	selects Clear option
Y	Yes, to confirm

Now you are ready to load the worksheet into the memory. To do this,

Place the data diskette from which you wish to load into Drive A.

Leave your cursor on any location and type:

T	starts TRANSFER command
L	selects Load option

Type in the name of the file you wish to load.

RETURN	executes the command

_____ **NOTE** _____

Remember, never enter values into cells containing formulas, or the formulas will be erased.

_____

CHAPTER NINETEEN

CONSIDERING A HUGE POPULATION WITH A LARGE SAMPLING

DESCRIPTION

When considering a large sampling which has been taken from a huge population, you must first decide on the degree of certainty you wish to obtain when calculating the range in which the population mean will lie. It is also necessary to restore the randomness of your population, because when you test the items in a sampling you remove them from the population and they cannot be returned after testing.

Then, based on the population size, the size of the sampling, the mean lifetime of the sample, the standard deviation of the population and the degree of certainty you desire, you can calculate the upper and lower limit for the actual population mean.

EXAMPLE

The Nantucket Manufacturing Company regularly tests the light bulbs which it manufactures. In their latest test, the company took a sampling of 100 light bulbs out of its last batch of 5000. The degree of certainty they seek is 95%. The sample mean lifetime is 175 hours, and the standard deviation of the population is 18 hours.

The company wants to determine the upper and lower limits for the actual population mean. They also need to know the actual quantity, with the randomness restored after removal of the sample items.

SETTING UP YOUR WORKSHEET - ENTERING LABELS

USE THE FOLLOWING STEP-BY-STEP DIRECTIONS FOR ENTERING THE LABELS IN FIGURE 1:

First expand column 1 so that it will accommodate the length of your labels.

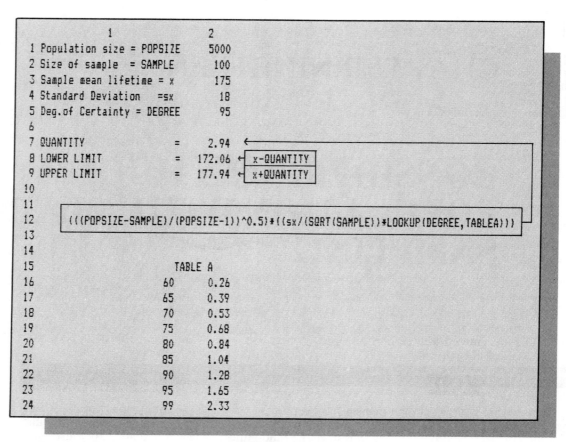

Figure 1

To do this, place your cursor on column 1 and type:

F	starts FORMAT command
W	selects Width option
25	width of column
RETURN	executes the command

_____ **NOTE** _____

Before typing in labels, you must first type:

A   starts ALPHA command which prepares the cell for labeling information

Then type in the label.

RETURN   enters label

Now type in your labels.

Next type in "Table A" and its values at the bottom of your worksheet.

After you have typed in "Table A," you will name it, because you will be using it later in a formula.

To name "Table A,"

Place your cursor on R16C1 and type:

N	starts NAME command
TABLEA	name given to table
TAB	moves cursor to R16C1, upper left-hand corner of table to be named
:	colon - indicates from-to
R24C2	lower right-hand corner of table to be named
RETURN	executes the command

After you have entered all the labels, as well as the values in Table A at the bottom of your worksheet, you will begin entering the known values and naming their locations.

ENTERING AND NAMING VALUES

USE THE FOLLOWING STEP-BY-STEP DIRECTIONS FOR ENTERING AND NAMING THE KNOWN VALUES.

___ **NOTE** ___

Naming of cells or groups of cells where values or formulas are placed is only done to make it easier to describe the cells' locations when used in formulas. If you don't name the cells, you can type in the address or point to the cell for cell identification.

Once a cell or group of cells is named, the name remains, regardless of any labels, values or formulas that may be entered into that location.

In this exercise, we have taken the option of naming some of our cells in order to make the construction of the formula(s) easier to understand.

The first value to enter, in column 2, to the right of Popsize, is the population size.

Place your cursor on R1C2 and type:

5000	population size
RETURN	enters the value

Now you will name the cell into which you have just entered the value.

Leave your cursor on R1C2 and type:

N	starts NAME command
POPSIZE	name given to cell
RETURN	executes the command

The second value, in column 2, to the right of sample, is the size of the sample.

Plae your cursor on R2C2 and type:

100	size of sample
RETURN	enters the value

Now you will name the cell into which you have just entered the value.

Leave your cursor on R2C2 and type:

N	starts NAME command
SAMPLE	name given to cell
RETURN	executes the command

The third value, in column 2, to the right of x, is the sample mean lifetime.

Place your cursor on R3C2 and type:

175	sample mean lifetime
RETURN	enters the value

Now name the cell into which you have just entered the value.

Leave your cursor on R3C2 and type:

N	starts NAME command
x	name given to cell
RETURN	executes the command

The fourth value, in column 2, to the right of sx, is the standard deviation of population.

Place your cursor on R4C2 and type:

18	standard deviation of population
RETURN	enters the value

Now you will name the cell into which you have just entered the value.

Leave your cursor on R4C2 and type:

N   starts NAME command

sx   name given to cell

RETURN   executes the command

The fifth value, in column 2, to the right of degree, is the degree of certainty (95%, found in column 1 in Table A below).

Place your cursor on R5C2 and type:

95   degree of certainty

RETURN   enters the value

You will now name the cell into which you have just entered the value.

Leave your cursor on R5C2 and type:

N   starts NAME command

DEGREE   name given to cell

RETURN   executes the command

Now that you have entered all the known values, you will enter the formulas.

ENTERING FORMULAS

USE THE FOLLOWING STEP-BY-STEP DIRECTIONS FOR ENTERING THE FORMULAS WHICH WILL CALCULATE THE UNKNOWN VALUES, and name them if the values generated by them are needed in another formula.

Formula one, in column 2, to the right of Quantity, restores the randomness of your selection.

Place your cursor on R7C2 and type:

(((POPSIZE-SAMPLE)/(POPSIZE-1))^0.5)*((sx/(SQRT(SAMPLE))*LOOKUP(DEGREE,TABLEA)))

RETURN   enters the formula

You now need to format the cell so that it will be displayed with two decimal places. To do this,

Leave your cursor on R7C2 and type:

F   starts FORMAT command

C   selects Cells option and displays R7C2

TAB TAB   moves cursor to Format Code:

F   selects Fixed option

TAB	moves cursor to # of decimals:
2	number of decimal places
RETURN	executes the command

You will now name the cell into which you have just entered the formula.

Leave your cursor on R7C2 and type:

N	starts NAME command
QUANTITY	name given to cell
RETURN	executes the command

Formula two, in column 2, to the right of Lower Limit, calculates the lower limit for the actual population mean.

Place your cursor on R8C2 and type:

V	starts VALUE command
x-QUANTITY	formula
RETURN	enters the formula

You now need to format the cell so that it will be displayed with two decimal places. To do this,

Leave your cursor on R8C2 and type:

F	starts FORMAT command
C	selects Cells option and displays R8C2
TAB TAB	moves cursor to Format Code:
F	selects Fixed option
TAB	moves cursor to # of decimals:
2	number of decimal places
RETURN	executes the command

Formula three, in column 2, to the right of Upper Limit, calculates the upper limit for the actual population mean.

Place your cursor on R9C2 and type:

V	starts VALUE command
x+QUANTITY	formula
RETURN	enters the formula

You now need to format the cell so that it will be displayed with two decimal places. To do this,

Leave your cursor on R9C2 and type:

F	starts FORMAT command
C	selects Cells option and displays R9C2
TAB TAB	moves cursor to Format Code:
F	selects Fixed option
TAB	moves cursor to # of decimals:
2	number of decimal places
RETURN	executes the command

Now that you have entered all your values and formulas, and named them, your worksheet is complete and should look like Figure 1.

Now that your worksheet is complete, it is ready and all you need to do is enter your own set of known values.

_____ **NOTE** _____

Never enter values into cells containing formulas, or the formulas will be erased.

SAVING YOUR WORKSHEET

Now save your worksheet for future use, so that the next time you wish to figure these computations all you will need to do is enter in your new known values, and you will not need to retype in the labels or enter the formulas.

To save your worksheet, place a formatted data diskette in Drive A.

With your cursor on any location, type:

T	starts TRANSFER command
S	selects Save option

Type in name of file.

RETURN	executes the command

PRINTING YOUR WORKSHEET

To print your worksheet, type:

P   starts PRINT command

P   selects Print option and prints

_ NOTE _

If you wish to set an Epson printer to compressed font, type:

P   starts PRINT command

O   selects Options option

[TAB]   moves cursor to Setup:

ˆO   sets Epson printer to compressed font
                           Note: type **letter** O

[RETURN]   prepares for another option selection

P   selects Print option, and prints

LOADING YOUR WORKSHEET BACK INTO MULTIPLAN

At a later date, when you need to use the worksheet to do further computations, just load your worksheet back into memory.

To do this, you must first clear memory if there is anything in it. To clear the memory,

Leave your cursor on any location and type:

T   starts TRANSFER command

C   selects Clear option

Y   Yes, to confirm

Now you are ready to load the worksheet into the memory. To do this,

Place the data diskette from which you wish to load into Drive A.

Leave your cursor on any location and type:

T   starts TRANSFER command

L   selects Load option

Type in the name of the file you wish to load.

[RETURN]   executes the command

_ NOTE _

Remember, never enter values into cells containing formulas, or the formulas will be erased.

INDEX OF FUNCTIONS AND COMMANDS

(continued on next page)

INDEX OF FUNCTIONS AND COMMANDS
(continued)

Note: The functions and commands appear in more pages than listed in this index.

REFERENCES

Farish and Greynolds, et al, Calculator Analysis for Business and Finance

Grawoig, Fielitz, Robinson, and Tabor, Mathematics: A Foundation for Decisions

Greynolds, et al, Executive Calculator Guidebook

Horngren, Cost Accounting: A Managerial Emphasis

Kieso and Weygandt, Intermediate Accounting

Miller and Orr, A Model of the Demand for Money by Firms

Weston and Brigham, Essentials of Managerial Finance